COAST FISHING

The book for beginners

by
Bertie Cox and Ryan Shellard

Published by Qué Book Publishing
Copyright © Bertie Cox and Ryan Shellard 1991

The rights of Bertie Cox and Ryan Shellard to be identified as the authors of this Work have been asserted by them in accordance with sections 77 and 78 of the Copyright, Design and Patents Act 1988.

Layout by Kay Williams, www.quedesign.co.uk
Illustrations by Bertie Cox

All rights reserved. This book or any portion thereof may not be reproduced or used in any manner whatsoever without the express written permission of the publisher except for the use of brief quotations in a book review.

1st edition (hardback): 1991; revised digital edition: 2012
2nd edition (paperback): 2016

CONTENTS

Introduction	Page 1
List of Illustrations	Page 2
Chapter 1 – Tackle	Page 5
Chapter 2 – Waters	Page 39
Chapter 3 – Fish	Page 45
Chapter 4 – Method	Page 75
Chapter 5 – Hints and Tips	Page 93

INTRODUCTION

The wonderful thing about coarse fishing is that you can begin at any age. From eight to eighty-eight. If you are very inexperienced you can catch fish with the lightest and simplest of tackle. As you progress you can add roach poles, bait trays, baitpults, electronic bite detectors and as much sophistication as you can carry to the water's edge. And then with the wisdom and consideration of experience you can return to that favourite swim with the very minimum of equipment and still enjoy the exhilaration of the 'rod-bender'. The basics of everything you need to know are in this simple to understand and incredibly comprehensive little book.

LIST OF ILLUSTRATIONS

Figure 1 – Stand-off rod ring
Figure 2 – Fixed spool reel
Figure 3 – Line on the spool
Figure 4 – Closed face reel
Figure 5 – Parts of a hook
Figure 6 – Spade end whipping knot
Figure 7 – Blood knot
Figure 8 – Treble hook
Figure 9 – Split shot
Figure 10 – Bullet weight
Figure 11 – Coffin weight
Figure 12 – Ledger bomb
Figure 13 – Swimfeeders
Figure 14 – Plummet
Figure 15 – Landing nets
Figure 16 – Rod rests
Figure 17 – Floats
Figure 18 – Disgorger
Figure 19 – Swivels
Figure 20 – Features of a fish
Figure 21 – Barbel
Figure 22 – Bleak
Figure 23 – Bream
Figure 24 – Carp (Common)
Figure 25 – Carp (Leather)

Figure 26 – Carp (Mirror)
Figure 27 – Carp (Crucian)
Figure 28 – Catfish
Figure 29 – Chub
Figure 30 – Dace
Figure 31 – Eel
Figure 32 – Grayling
Figure 33 – Gudgeon
Figure 34 – Perch
Figure 35 – Pike
Figure 36 – Roach
Figure 37 – Rudd
Figure 38 – Ruffe
Figure 39 – Tench
Figure 40 – Zander
Figure 41 – Floats
Figure 42 – Ledger rigs
Figure 43 – Disgorger
Figure 44 – Plummet in use with hook
Figure 45 – Deadbait
Figure 46 – Spinner
Figure 47 – Spoon
Figure 48 – Plug
Figure 49 – Hooking of baits

Please note: none of the illustrations of equipment or fish are drawn to scale.

CHAPTER 1
TACKLE

RODS

There are various types of coarse fishing and different rods are used for each.

Float Rods

Like all other styles of rod, these are usually made of carbon fibre which is very strong, light and easy to handle. For beginners a rod of around ten to twelve feet in length (3-3.5m) is ideal for general float fishing.

When buying a float rod you must be sure that the rod rings are of the stand-off type. This ensures that the line remains clear of the rod when wet. These rod rings should be positioned fairly close together with space between them reducing towards the top of the rod.

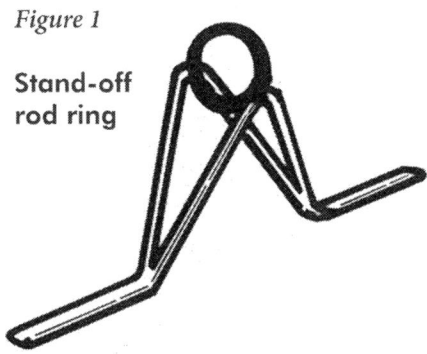

Figure 1

Stand-off rod ring

The length and thickness of the rod handle – or butt – are also very important. The length should not be so long that it protrudes so far behind your elbow that it is uncomfortable and upsets balance. The average ideal length for an adult is around 24 inches (.6m). It should also be of a manageable diameter. One inch (2.5cm) is about right.

The action of the rod is important and there are simple ways to test it when you go to buy one. Hold it horizontally as you will when you are fishing and point towards ground level. Strike upwards as if you were trying to connect with a fish and watch the reaction of the rod tip. If it bounces up and down too easily it really isn't a stiff enough action. Another good test is to get someone to hold the rod end at waist level while you slowly lift the rod upwards. You will then be able to see how the rod bends – whether the action is largely at the top, through the middle or throughout. Generally, for the inexperienced fisherman, the action should be at the top since it helps the speed of reaction to a bite.

Ledger rods

These usually now come in the form of quiver or feeder rods that are between ten and twelve feet long (3.05-3.7m). The top section of the rod, usually one to two feet in length (30cm-60cm) is called the quiver tip which is designed to bend or quiver when a fish samples or takes the bait. These rods are available with tip sections of varying degrees of stiffness or rigidity according to the type of fish you are targeting. Smaller, shyer species will require a more sensitive action, or 'test curve' as it is known, than bigger, more powerful species that need a much stiffer action. This style of bite detection is a popular and effective method when fishing on the bed of both still and running waters.

Spinning rods

As the description indicates these are to cast a spinner or lure (*see page 85*). A general spinning rod is between eight and 10 feet long (2.5-3m) and probably constructed of a mixture of glass and carbon. Most often the main function of the rod is to provide strong and accurate distance casting and therefore should be of a stiff action. A loose or floppy action will mean inaccurate or even unmanageable casting. The handle can be relatively short since one is not holding the rod in one position for any length of time and is usually retrieving the line immediately after casting. In general when spinning, one is going for larger fighting fish and a stiff action rod will assist in casting, playing and landing. There are many types of more specialist spinning rods which you can learn about as you become more proficient in the sport.

Poles

These are closest to the very original concept of coarse fishing when it was simply a question of a stick, a line, a bent pin and a worm.

The main uses of a pole are for accurate placement of float and bait where general casting would be difficult. For example a small gap in lily pads or weed which would be virtually impossible to cast into with the conventional use of a reel or where the current is so strong one needs a method of holding the float and bait in the same place.

There are two basic types of pole. The first is the 'take apart' variety with which the angler removes each tapered section, shortening the pole to a manageable length to land the fish at the water's edge. The second type of pole is telescopic, each section being twisted gently to slide into the wider section below, again reducing the length. Since this is a beginner's guide to coarse fishing we will only discuss the telescopic type, normally constructed of a carbon and fibre glass mix. These are easier to use, considerably cheaper than the take apart type, and the easy action offers more bend throughout the overall length of the rod which can be an advantage when bringing in a good fish.

The simplest method of pole fishing is the 'flick tip' method. The line is tied directly to the small ring or nylon loop at the tip of the pole. The line with terminal tackle (float, weights and baited hook) is then simply swung out over the water. The longer the pole the further across the water you can reach. A good general purpose pole is between 17 and 20 feet (5-6m) but a shorter length of between 10 and 14 feet (3-4m) can be particularly useful for the very young or inexperienced who have not yet mastered the use of a reel.

REELS

The whole object of a reel is to be able to control the casting and retrieval of line. In many respects the choice of a reel in coarse fishing is as important as the rod selection.

Fixed Spool Reels

The most generally used reel is the fixed spool type which, since its conception, has revolutionised coarse angling. This style of reel offers the smoothest and least resistant method of getting line off the spool resulting in longer and easier casting plus the fastest method of retrieval. It is false economy to buy at the lower end of the price ranges. Cheap reels can present an awful lot of aggravation. Not only are they less sturdy but there is a good chance they will cause all sorts of problems, particularly to the inexperienced angler. There can be little more frustrating than line caught in the mechanism behind the spool, the bail arm sticking or failing to return, lack of good control of the clutch and dreadful tangles that can spoil precious angling time.

Figure 2 **Fixed spool reel**

When choosing a good all purpose reel look for the following:

Size: small to medium – with capacity to hold 100 yards (91.5m) of 2lbs/4lbs (.9-1.8kg) breaking strain monofilament line. Too small a spool and you may not have enough line capacity particularly if ledgering. Too large and you'll have to pack out the spool with tape or much more line so that when the final 100 yards (91.5m) of line is on, the spool is loaded to the correct level to maximise casting performance.

Figure 3 **Line on spool**

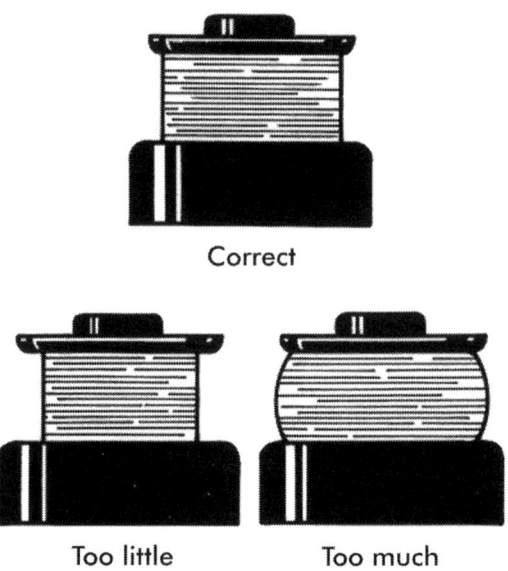

Correct

Too little   Too much

Gear Ratio: this is the rate at which the reel will retrieve the line. A ratio of 3:1 means that when the handle is rotated one full turn, the bail arm rotates 3 times – retrieving approximately 15 inches (38cm) with each turn of the reel handle. When choosing your first reel you should be looking for one that can provide good general performance in all types of coarse fishing. An ideal gear ratio for this is 4:1.

The Drag: all modern reels have a fully adjustable drag. The drag normally consists of two discs that rub together slowing the speed of the rotating spool and thus slowing the rate at which line is released. In simple terms the drag acts like a brake and its tension should be set according to the breaking strain of the line. The drag is used to give you greater control when playing a large fish. Should the fish lunge away you will need to provide line for it to run, whilst keeping it under firm control.

Anti Reverse: all fixed spool and closed face reels have an anti-reverse lock to stop the spool spinning, thus releasing line, when a fish takes the bait.

Closed Face Reels

Basically a very similar concept to the fixed spool with most of its features. The main difference is that instead of a bail arm a rotating metal cup fits over the spool. The cup carries a stud around which the line is fed. A second metal cup fits over the inner one which rotates, retrieving the line. To allow the line to run free the stud is retracted by the use of a release catch.

Figure 4 **Closed face reel**

Centre Pins

These are the forerunners of all reels and, whilst the simplest of design, are probably nowadays the most difficult to use effectively, particularly if long casting is required.

The centre pin is a flanged drum of between 3" to 5" (7.6-12.7cm) diameter which holds the line and spins freely on an axle. They are normally built with an anti reverse mechanism and some even have a drag facility similar to the Fixed Spool type.

One distinct advantage of a centre pin is that it allows float tackle to drift smoothly with the current since the spool can turn freely with minimum pull from the line.

Quick retrieval of the line can be achieved by a strong spin of the drum or a handle provided for steady, controlled retrieve. If as a beginner you can only afford one reel then it must be of the fixed spool variety – not a centre pin.

LINE

The most common type and almost exclusively used now is nylon monofilament. It is available in breaking strains from four ounces (113g) to 130 pounds (59kg). It has become so popular since it stretches to absorb the tension of striking or playing a fish and minimises the possibility of snapping under stress.

As one general purpose line for the beginner a breaking strain of between 3lbs and 4lbs (1.3-1.8kg) should suffice. Any knots you make by mistake in the line should be removed – even if it means discarding that whole length, as a knot becomes the weakest spot and most likely breaking point.

TRACES

If you are fishing for pike or zander you should use a metal trace between the line and hook or lure as these fish have sharp teeth that can tear through nylon. Traces are available in various lengths and breaking strains normally with a quick release and attach clip at one end for the lure and a swivel at the other for tying to the reel line.

HOOKS

There is a vast selection of coarse fishing hooks not to mention the many different sizes. *And just to confuse you – the smaller the hook, the larger its size number!* Broadly, a size 22 is probably as small as you'll ever need to buy for fishing with a single maggot or caster. (A caster, or

Figure 5 **Parts of a hook**

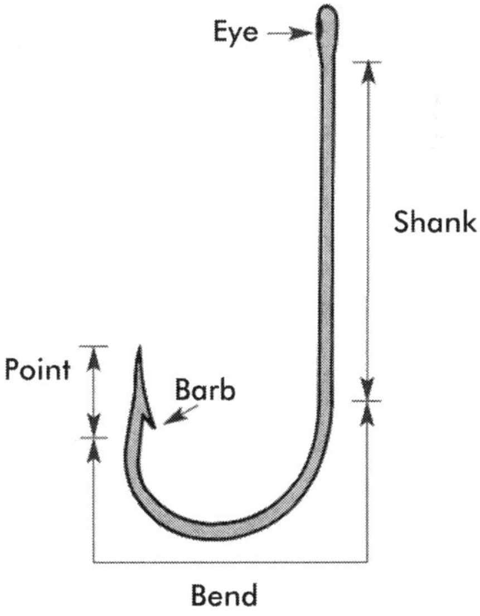

chrysalis as it was once more commonly known, is the stage where a maggot develops a crispy shell which gradually turns brown before hatching into a bluebottle fly.) A size 12 is about right for a piece of sweetcorn, a brandling worm (a species of earthworm which has adapted to flourishing in decaying organic material such as rotting vegetation, compost and manure – they are rarely found in soil), or a piece of cheese. Then you can go to bigger sizes for lumps of bread flake (simply fresh bread squeezed round the hook) and so on.

NB: Figure 5 shows a 'barbed' hook but virtually all managed waters now insist on the use of barbless hooks and some illustrations throughout the rest of this book show the latter.

There are far too many hook styles to go into detail in this book but the following is a brief description of the basic types you will need:

Spade end hooks are flattened into a spade shape at the top of the shank and are whipped to nylon by the angler as shown in Figure 6.

Eyed hooks are supplied with a ring at the top of the shank and are whipped to the nylon reel line or hook length using a variety of knots. An easy and effective knot is shown in Figure 7 on page 16.

Hooks to nylon are supplied already tied to a short length of nylon – called the hook length – of appropriate breaking strain with a loop at the end to which the reel line is tied. Hook sizes are indicated by even numbers from 2 to 30. The larger the number the smaller the hook.

As a general rule hook sizes of between 12 and 22, the size

Figure 6 **Spade end whipping knot**

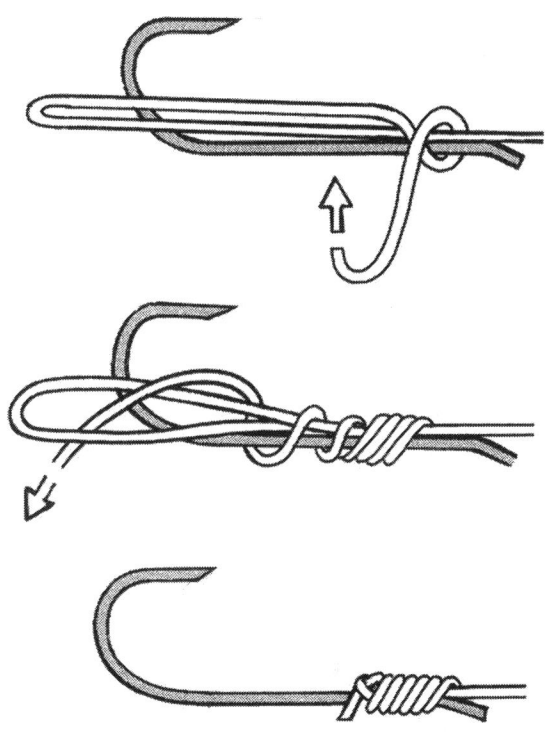

depending on the bait being used, are adequate for most fish up to four pounds (1.8kg). That isn't to say that a ten pound (4.5kg) carp cannot be successfully landed using a size 20 hook!

For fishing with maggot a short shanked hook is most suitable whilst if using bigger baits such as bread, lobworms, sweetcorn, cheese etc, then a longer shanked hook is desirable. As little as possible of the hook should be showing when baited as long as the point protrudes: i.e. – a size 12 hook with a single maggot is much less likely to

Figure 7 **Blood knot**

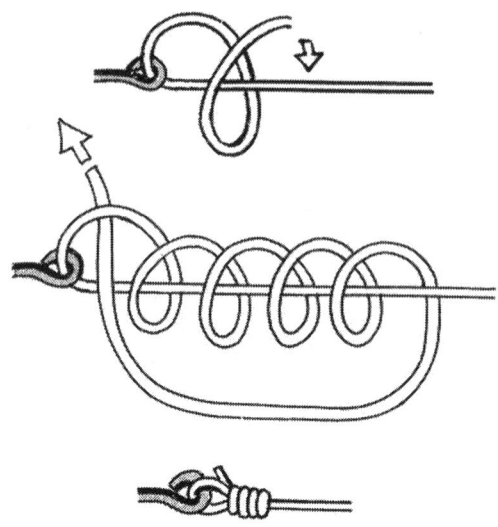

attract fish than a size 18, 20 or 22 because of the smallness of the bait and the amount of hook visible. Wide bend hooks are now available which are ideal to allow you to present a piece of sweetcorn or other chunkier baits more naturally.

Barbs *(see Figure 5 on page 14)*. Many fisheries now understandably insist on the use of barbless hooks. One downside of this for a beginner is that it does slightly increase the chance of losing the fish whilst landing it since it may twist, turn and slip the hook. However, the very important upside is that, once landed, it is much easier to remove the hook without injury to the fish. And most importantly the fish can be returned to the water much more quickly and without damage. Never use rusting hooks as they may have become brittle and could snap.

Treble hooks are normally mounted on plugs, lures or spinners which are used for large, powerful, fighting fish such as pike, chub, perch or zander. They can also be used for deadbaiting (*see page 84*) for any of the above.

Figure 8 **Treble hook**

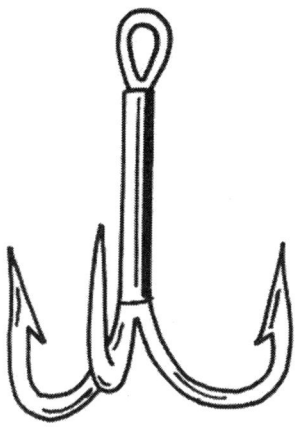

WEIGHTS

The most environmentally important fact regarding coarse fishing weights is that the traditional lead weight has been banned in the UK at all sizes up to one ounce (28.3g). Now, all weights must be non-toxic and lead-free. The effect of lead upon wild life, particularly swans, has been devastating. Thousands of swans were dying annually of lead poisoning through angling and shooting. Swans have to take grit into their gizzards to help crush their food before digestion and they had been taking in the lost or discarded lead shot from anglers and the pellets from shotgun cartridges.

Split shot – so called because it is a tiny ball of non-toxic metal mix with a slot cut more than half way through.

Figure 9 **Split shot**

The line is inserted into this and the shot is squeezed onto it to hold it in the required position below the float. The shot must not be squeezed with more than finger pressure as the line may be damaged which will result in a weak point and possibly line breakage.

Also, you need to be able to open up the shot after fishing, to be able to keep it for re-use next time.

The purpose of split shot is to weight the float so it 'cocks' and sits upright in the water and the bait is taken to the required depth. This is dealt with in detail in Chapter 4 under 'floats'. Split shot sizes range from dust shot little bigger than a pinhead – all the way through numerous sizes up to SSG (swan shot) which are just fifteen to the ounce (28.3g).

When buying your first selection of split shot, the simplest plan is to buy a dispenser that contains a good mix of all sizes.

Ledger weights These are most commonly used when no

float is employed and a static bait on the bed of the water is required – again this technique is explained in Chapter 4. Lead free ledger bombs are made from steel, brass or zinc. They are available in various sizes and shapes for different ledgering methods.

- **The bullet** (ball shaped) with a hole in the centre for the line to pass through is used to roll along the bottom with the current to present a naturally drifting bait.

Figure 10 **Bullet weight**

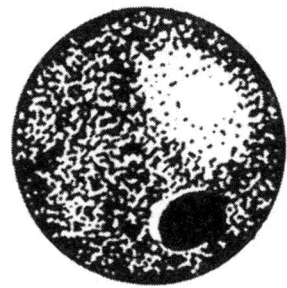

- **The coffin** shaped weight – again with a hole through its centre for the line – is designed to lie flat on the bed of the water to hold the bait stationary in the flow.

Figure 11 **Coffin weight**

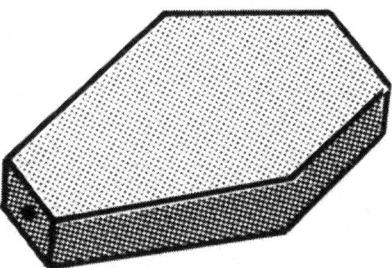

- **The Bomb** is usually a pear shaped weight with a swivel and a ring permanently fixed in the narrow end, or one that can be unscrewed from the weight to allow another of a different size to be screwed in. This type will sit firmly on the bottom with the line running freely through the ring.

Figure 12 **Ledger bomb**

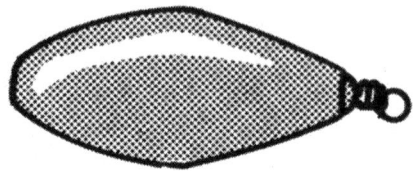

Ledger weights are held in place by a split shot positioned immediately below them to stop them sliding down to the hook. Usually about 8 inches (20cm) from the hook.

- **Swimfeeder.** A plastic cylinder with holes all around it and weighted as shown below.

    There is a removable lid at one end. The purpose is to loose feed groundbait, usually maggots, in close proximity to the hook bait on the bottom. The cylinder is packed with maggots and the lid replaced. It is then set up on the

Figure 13 **Swimfeeder**

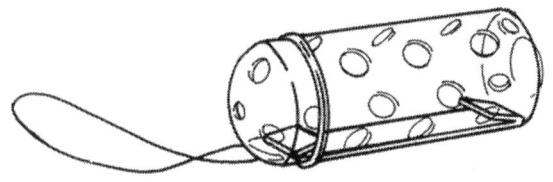

hook length in the same way as a regular ledger tackle. The weight in the cylinder works in place of the ledger bomb or other types of weight for casting and holding it on the bottom. The maggots crawl out of the holes in the cylinder close to your hook bait. The swimfeeder can be fished fixed or free, running on the line in the same way as the conventional ledger and should be positioned around 12 inches (30cm) from the hook.

Open ended swimfeeders are also available for cereal or bread groundbaits which are released from the cylinder by water movement. These groundbaits can also be laced with maggot or caster when being packed into the swimfeeder.

- **The Plummet** is a flat based, bomb shaped weight with a cork strip running across the bottom. This is used for determining the depth of the water you are fishing. How to do this is explained in Chapter 4, page 83.

Figure 14 **Plummet**

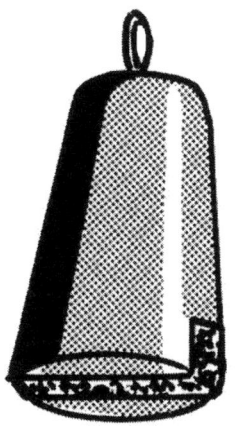

NETS

There are two types of net that the coarse angler normally carries – a landing net which is a very vital piece of tackle and a keep net which is less important unless you are match fishing.

Landing nets

There are many types for specialist fishing. They range from shallow trays with long telescopic handles for the smaller regular coarse fish to very deep nets of up to 42 inches (1.2m) diameter to safely capture the largest specimen fish.

Frames are constructed of either alloy or glass fibre and are of circular or triangular design. They are usually collapsible for easy transport and have a screw thread for attachment to the handle.

The latest of both these types of net can now be purchased made of rubber which is very useful. The rubber mesh is non-absorbent and therefore the smell of fish on the netting is eradicated – no more smelly tackle bag! Also hooks tend not to penetrate the rubber which can save them getting caught in the material.

There are a number of gauges of mesh. Wide mesh netting is not advised since small fish can get caught in it by their gills and it can also damage fish by fins getting entangled.

Micromesh, or close to it, is best for a general coarse fishing net.

The triangular style of net is most popular since it offers one wide straight side on the edge the fish is drawn over

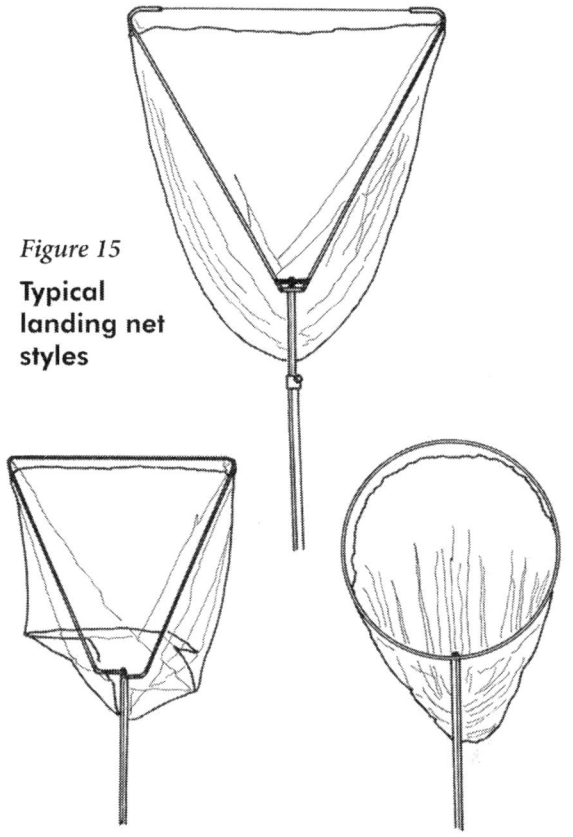

Figure 15

Typical landing net styles

which helps prevent the fish being able to slip around the edge of a circular one.

A general all-purpose net should have a depth of between 12 and 18 inches (30-45cm).

A good general duty handle is of the telescopic type in either 2 or 3 sections in metal or carbon fibre. They are supplied with a universal screw thread for any type of net. The two section version is normally made in metal and adjusted for length by a locking screw thread which gives infinitely variable lengths.

The three section type, also usually in carbon fibre, is adjusted section by section with a twist grip action, similar to the pole rod discussed earlier under 'rods'. Either of these is quite adequate for the beginner and will continue to be of good service for many years.

Keep nets

These are obviously a must for the match angler who has to weigh in with his total catch at the end of a competition but many pleasure anglers also enjoy seeing and possibly photographing their bag of fish at the end of the day. It is obviously imperative to keep the caught fish in the best condition to be able to safely release them back to the water and the keep net must facilitate this.

The net should be either of minnowmesh or micromesh gauge. The finer the mesh, the less the fish can be damaged in any way. Similar to the landing net a wide mesh could cause a fish to get stuck by its gills or cause damage to fins. Keep nets come in a circular or rectangular design. The main advantage of the rectangular type is that if fishing in shallow water it offers the maximum area to lie on the bed of the water and thus more water space for the fish within.

The circular type is most popular and it is worth buying one of large diameter and the greatest depth you can afford. If you have had to fish deep for your catch it is only fair to keep the fish in the conditions they prefer. For instance, a shallow net may cause the fish to be retained in water temperatures to which they are not best suited. Also, if the fishing has been good too many fish retained in too small an area could cause them damage.

Pike or Zander should not be retained in a keep net as they may well bite at and damage the net and no large predatory fish should be retained in the net where there are other small fish on which they could dine! Also, generally Carp should not be kept in a keep net since the first two or three spines of their dorsal fin are much tougher than most other species and could get caught up in the mesh. Special sacks can be purchased for holding carp which is covered a little later on.

In a flowing water a keep net should be positioned so that the majority of the sub surface area is pointing downstream. This allows the retained fish maximum water space to face into the current as they would normally.

It is useful to attach some sort of heavy weight to the bottom of the keep net to ensure it stays stretched out to its maximum depth. If this is difficult to do at the water's edge you could put a heavy stone inside the net which will have the same effect. If you use this method great care should be exercised when hauling the net up with fish in it so that the stone doesn't roll around and damage them.

The top ring is supplied with a universal screw thread to attach to a bank stick – a light alloy, pointed pole of around 3 to 4 feet (.9-1.2m) which is driven into the ground so that the opening of the keep net is conveniently close to you when you begin to fish.

The top ring of the net should be of the plastic coated variety so that should a fish come in contact with it when being placed in the net, it cannot be damaged.

Maintenance

Keep nets should be checked regularly for any signs of fraying or small breaks in the mesh caused by lifting from unseen underwater obstacles or bankside bushes and branches.

They should always be thoroughly washed out with clean water as fish slime will build up on the mesh causing it to become abrasive and possibly damaging to fish. Unwashed nets can become unpleasantly smelly, particularly after a period of storage. More importantly, unclean nets – landing and keep nets – could possibly transfer any diseases from one water to another. Much of the above is eradicated with the use of rubber mesh nets mentioned earlier in this section. Most stillwater fisheries now require ALL nets (landing and keep nets) to be properly dipped in a tank of antiseptic solution provided, before and after fishing.

Keep Net Regulations

Many water authorities specify a minimum size of net to be used, as do most clubs, some of whom even state the number of fish of any species that may be retained at any one time. In fact many stillwater fisheries now only allow the use of keep nets during competitions.

SACKS

Made of rot-proof nylon with holes for water to pass through. They can be tied at the neck so the fish retained can see nothing and therefore does not feel it has any chance of escape. This is important for a very large fish that may have become exhausted during the process of being caught, after which it will need a period of time to rest and regain its strength. Large carp, pike and barbel for instance which have fought hard can be severely damaged or even die if released immediately back into the water where they will swim away in panic, or retained in a regular net where they will continue to try and escape. Sacks are only needed by specialist specimen hunters and are not a tackle item carried by the average angler.

ROD RESTS

In most methods of angling rod rests are used constantly. In float fishing one needs to have two free hands to apply bait, groundbait or even eat lunch. In ledgering it is important for bite detection that the rod remains perfectly still which is virtually impossible if hand held. Usually two rests are employed to position the rod so that its tip is only inches from the surface of the water.

Figure 16 **Rod rests**

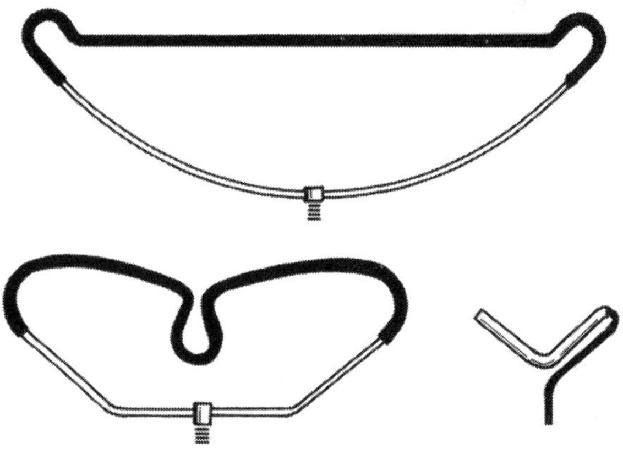

Like so many tackle items there are many designs of rod rests to choose from. Within this book we have confined our illustration above to the more standard types which will cover the needs of a regular coarse angler.

BANK STICKS

These are simply alloy poles supplied in a variety of lengths, some even being telescopic. They all have a pointed end for ease of pushing into the ground and a universal screw thread at the top to be able to fix rod rests, bait trays or keep nets.

BITE INDICATORS

The simplest and most obvious detection method is the line suddenly moving through or across the water. This is most likely to show a fish has taken the bait and is moving off with it. But this is only possible on a perfectly still water without a breath of wind and with conditions that are likely to stay that way – which of course is extremely unlikely. Therefore, some method must be employed to see when a fish is interested in, or has taken the bait you have presented. The methods are numerous depending on the depth of fishing, the distance, still, slow or fast moving waters.

Floats

The most common coarse fishing bite detector particularly for beginners is the float. These, like so many aspects of tackle, are available in many styles for a variety of applications, some of which are illustrated in Figure 17.

The float is weighted so that it 'cocks' to a vertical position with only the minimum amount visible above the surface at whatever distance you have cast depending on the water conditions – i.e. if it is choppy, you need to see sufficient of the float so that it doesn't disappear from view in the ripples or the waves. The basic principle of the float is that it will react in some way when a fish expresses interest in or takes the bait. The less of the float there is visible above the water, the less resistance the fish will feel as it takes the bait. The section on Float Fishing in Chapter 4 covers the various types of float movement you can expect.

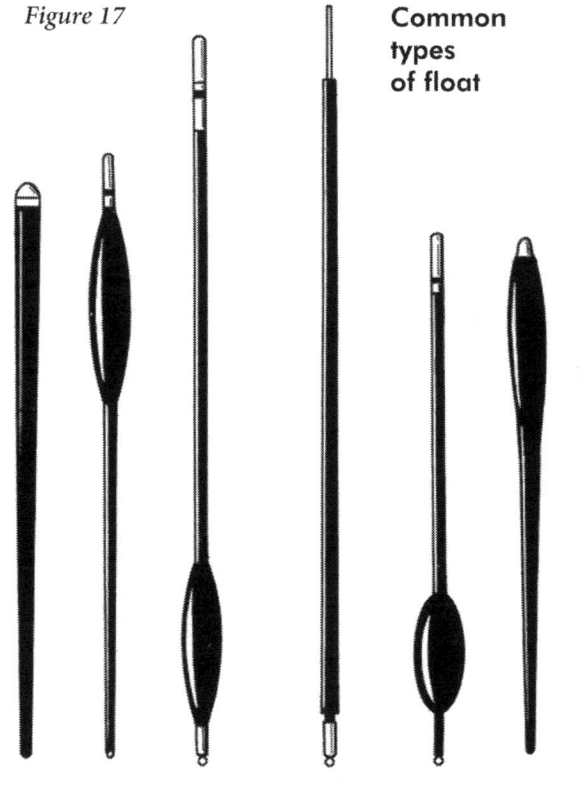

Figure 17 **Common types of float**

Stick   Avon   Zoomer   Waggler   Onion   Balsa

Quiver Tip

As already mentioned at the beginning of this book under 'rods', the quiver tip is an integral part of the quiver or feeder rod. It is the top section of the rod and is designed to bend or quiver whenever a fish is tasting or has taken your bait. These tip sections are available in different 'test curves' or degrees of stiffness or rigidity, depending on the size and power of the species you are likely to catch.

When stillwater fishing, after casting, the rod should be placed at 90 degrees to where you have cast your bait and the quiver tip should be close to the water to reduce any movement of it caused by wind. On moving water, such as rivers, the quiver tip should be pointing in the direction of your cast but lifted and creating tension between the tip and your weight and bait which will reduce the effect on the line from any current.

Bobbins/Monkey Climbers

A bobbin is a method of bite detection in many ways similar to other types of ledgering but instead of being at the rod tip is placed between the reel and the first ring on the rod. You can make them yourself from something as simple as a small piece of bread flake or cheese squeezed on to the line, a piece of aluminium foil (chewing gum wrapper?) or anything that can be easily hooked over the line that will either fall off or be easily removed when striking a bite.

But proper angling bobbins are available at tackle dealers and are often adjustable for weight.

The method is simply to create a 'V' in the line between reel and first ring which will be drawn up level to the rod when a fish moves away with the bait.

If the weather is blustery and there is a likelihood of the bobbin being blown around, the monkey climber offers a more stable solution. This is simply a slim alloy pole of around 2 feet (.6m) long that is pushed into the ground. Over this slides a plastic mechanism known as the monkey that hooks over the line. This is then slid down the pole to a chosen position and remains thus until a bite is detected by the upward movement of the monkey on the pole. As the strike is carried out the monkey rides to the top and off the pole thus releasing the line.

Electronic Bite Detectors

The principle of this type of bite detection is similar to those of other ledgering methods as detailed above, the difference being that these offer an audible signal as opposed to a visual one. A battery powered unit is screwed on to a bank stick or clipped directly on to the rod rest and the line is inserted into a channel in the detector under a pressure sensitive switch in the form of a wire. When a fish takes the bait the line lifts upwards touching the wire which in turn is lifted creating the completion of a circuit within the detector which sets off an audible signal.

These, of course, are far more expensive than other ledgering methods discussed but are nevertheless invaluable for night fishing when visual techniques are normally impossible.

GENERAL TACKLE

The tackle detailed so far may appear to be all you could need to catch fish but this section is equally essential to be able to enjoy the sport, protect fish and be comfortably efficient for problem free fishing. Many of the smaller items featured here are inexpensive, will last a lifetime with proper care and soon become indispensable.

Disgorgers

Available in plastic or alloy, they come in a number of sizes depending on the hook size being used and are for extracting a hook that is deeper in the fish's mouth or throat than can be safely removed using one's fingers. Good fishing techniques and experience should alleviate the use of a disgorger to a large extent but nevertheless it is an extremely important piece of tackle. (See Chapter 4 for detailed use.)

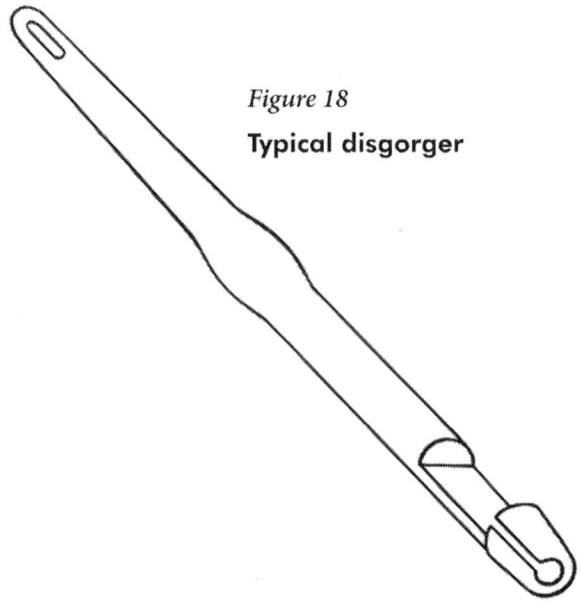

Figure 18

Typical disgorger

Forceps

Basically long slim pliers that lock, to attach to any deeply imbedded hook that cannot be removed with the fingers or disgorger. Large, tough-mouthed fish such as carp and barbel can present a problem and forceps will remove the hook without damage. Pike and Zander have extremely sharp pharyngeal teeth and forceps will save damage – possibly to the angler too!

Baitpults

If you are fishing, say, 20 yards (18m) out from the bank, it would not be easy to accurately place a ball of groundbait or a handful of boilies and it would be virtually impossible to spread a scattering of maggots on the chosen spot. A baitpult is quite simply a catapult designed with a bigger pouch to fire groundbaits accurately. It takes a little practice to become inch perfect but is an invaluable accessory when fishing at a distance. When purchasing make sure you feel comfortable with the power of the elastic and buy one with a good sized pouch and wide forks.

Scales

By no means an imperative piece of equipment but frustrating if you don't have them when you think you might have landed a really good sized fish. They should be very sensitive – ounces/grams count! – and you must take care to keep them cleaned and oiled to avoid them sticking, rusting and becoming inaccurate. An 11lb (5kg) maximum weight limit should suffice but if you believe you are going to be catching specimen sizes you can buy much more powerful ones, but these are likely to be far less sensitive to the smaller weights.

Fluorescent Float Tops

You can buy floats that have in-built fluorescent tops which you can use throughout the day and continue with after dusk with excellent visibility but these are extremely expensive. A cheaper alternative is to buy packets of fluorescent tops that are simply fixed to the successful float that you have been using throughout the day. With these tops, bending the plastic tube cracks the inner container within which chemicals combine to create a fluorescent glow. This tube is then pushed or taped on to your existing float top to give you a clearly visible night bite detector for up to 12 hours.

Bread Punches

A simple device to effectively drill a small piece of fresh bread out of a slice or loaf and apply the hook into it. By no means essential but simply a quick way of baiting with bread.

Swivels

These have free turning eyes, or rings, at both ends. They are a good method of linking line or a multi-strand trace to the main line since very secure knots can be tied to them. A swivel can also be useful as an anti tangle device when placed between the main line and the hook length to stop the hook swinging around the ledger weight, particularly during a fast retrieve. A drilled plastic bead through which the line passes is useful between the ledger and the swivel to protect the knot.

Figure 19 **Swivels**

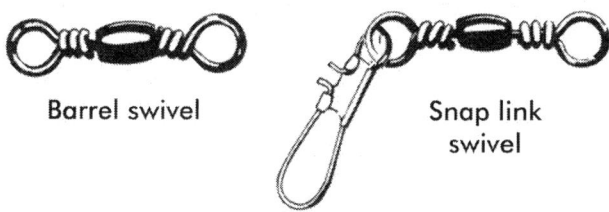

Barrel swivel   Snap link swivel

Bait Pots

Not even necessary to buy if you have any plastic containers with secure lids through which you can punch tiny air holes, but in any case they are not expensive. It is worth having 2 or 3 bait pots in various sizes. If you are going fishing for a morning you may feel half a pint of maggots is sufficient. A longer session, more maggots, bigger pot. You may want to dispense other baits such as sweetcorn or gather worms before you set out. And, of course, you could well want something in which to mix groundbait.

Tackle Container

Normally of plastic there are a variety of sizes and capacities. You could buy one simply for floats, disgorgers, hooks, ledger weights etc, or one that will contain your entire selection of equipment including reels.

Umbrellas

One of the more expensive items of equipment and heavy to carry, but we do live in Britain! They also make excellent wind breaks.

They are made of tough nylon or plastic and normally range from 36" to 54" (.9-1.4m) in diameter. The bigger the better in terms of keeping you and your tackle dry but bear in mind the extra weight you'll have to carry and the cost. They are usually supplied with a two section alloy pole, the inner of which is pointed at the base to push into the ground, while the other slides up or down and clips or screws to fix at the required height. Just below the umbrella spokes there is usually a swivel joint to allow you to adjust the angle. At the top centre on the outside of the umbrella there should be a ring to enable you to tie a string from it to a stake firmly driven into the ground to secure it on windy days.

Tackle Box

Let's be practical! First and foremost you'll want something to sit on so look for a sturdy frame with a cover and lid that makes a comfortable seat. Don't go for the very smallest because as you gain interest and experience in the sport you will collect more tackle and discover all sorts of things you want to take with you. But always remember that whatever you choose to take with you on a fishing trip, you could end up carrying it all for some distance and often over rough terrain, stiles etc.

The tackle box should have a comfortable, preferably padded shoulder strap and have a large pocket to hold the landing and keep nets.

Rod Bag

Make sure this has greater capacity than you are likely to need initially since you are almost certain to collect more rods. Check its length to ensure it will house your rod/s and still close securely. There should be a pocket for bank sticks but also check there is a pocket for your umbrella and landing net handle.

More expensive rod bags come with plastic tubes in which to put rods for protection – very useful if strapping the rod bag to a roof rack, using public transport or any situation where the rods could be exposed to being crushed.

Again be sure it has a comfortable preferably padded shoulder strap. Also, particularly for youngsters, check that the bag is not so long or the handle so placed that it is likely to drag on the ground while you are carrying it.

CHAPTER 2
WATERS

STILLWATERS

As a rule of thumb it is good to get to know one or two ponds or lakes well, as it can be taken that what happens within them is likely to be similar in unfamiliar waters.

In the forthcoming chapter on fish you will discover the species likely to be found in stillwaters along with their feeding habits and ways of seeing where they are likely to be feeding.

In this little book it won't be possible to detail all the ways of finding deep holes, the shallow, warmer lay-bys and the many other features that make up the contours of a pond or lake bed. Here we can only outline the most obvious hot spots and the 'reading of the water' in simple ways.

To begin with plummet the water (*see page 83*) to establish depths in the region you are planning to fish. The presence of water lilies and other floating plants are good areas to concentrate on in warmer weather. Many species lie in the shade they provide and predatory fish may move among them looking for an easy meal!

Bankside shrubs and bushes not only provide fish with shade and cover but can also supply natural foods such as insects and grubs that fall from them and berries and fruits at the relevant times of year.

Tree branches that become immersed in the water become covered in algae thus encouraging the larvae of aquatic insects and snails to collect thereon. Various species of fish will attend here to feed.

Surface bubbles, as mentioned where appropriate in the descriptions of each type of fish, can help greatly in discovering where they are feeding, but need to be studied. Natural detritus gases in the bottom layers of mud or silt can be released without disturbance by fish and send bubbles intermittently to the surface sometimes misleading the angler regarding the whereabouts of fish. Keep an eye out for moving plants or lilies on the surface. The movement could well be caused by large fish such as carp, tench or bream cruising between the subsurface foliage in search of food.

Small fish feeding can cause misleading splashes on the surface which in turn may gain the interest of a pike. Should that decide to dine there will be a frenzied surface activity of fleeing fish probably coupled with an audible and visible 'cloop' or splash as the Pike attacks its prey.

If there is no vegetation or other obvious clues to fish whereabouts another visual sign of activity may be a discolouration of the water in a particular area. This may well indicate that bottom feeding fish are foraging in the mud and silt of the bed sending clouds of it to the surface.

On large lakes, gravel pits and reservoirs that are unfamiliar your only chances of immediate success are either to talk to other anglers with experience of it or to study a map of the topography of its bed. In the absence of either of these the best option is to choose a bankside spot where you will be fishing directly into the wind. Surface insect life and plankton will have been blown in the direction of that shore where various species will congregate to feed.

For relaxation and enjoyment stillwaters provide a perfect

environment. They are often very attractive with overhanging trees and shrubs, lily pads, ducks, swans and other wildlife. And there is little more awe inspiring than a dawn mist over a silent pond on a summer morning or the sun setting between the trees, providing mirror-like reflections on a perfectly still water. For comfort of fishing still waters are second to none since it is normally easy to accurately cast to the same place each time with the minimal need for recasting as the bait is unlikely to move far from the chosen spot. Groundbaiting too is easy for the same reason and it is far less difficult, with care, to keep shoals in your swim for longer periods.

RUNNING WATERS

It is obvious that this covers an enormously broad spectrum of shapes and sizes of watercourses. From tiny babbling streams through slow sluggish rivers to main waterways with yacht and barge traffic. Broad, shallow, gravel or stony bottomed rivers. Clear, fast, muddy, deep, meandering or straight 'V' cut canals – the list is endless. Here we can only discuss in the broadest terms quick ways of reading a potential water and hopefully locating fish.

To begin with, if not visibly apparent, always plummet the water to establish depths. Plummeting a few locations in the swim will start to give you a picture of the river bed – i.e. whether there's a deceptive ledge just a few feet out in front of you, a deep gully or hole, or an area of shallow water.

Look for bends in the river where the pressure of the flow over centuries will have caused soil erosion on the outer bank of the bend and in all probability have created a deep run. The inner curve is likely to be much shallower. Providing the flow is not too severe, there is a good chance that fish will congregate and feed in this deep run.

A bay in the bank of an otherwise regular river course is known as a lay-by. Here the water tends to be slack where fish can lie in rest or wait for foods passing by in the main flow. These are particularly good fishing in winter when the main course of the river is likely to be of a greater flow and the lay-by full and weed free.

Eddies are often caused by clashing currents, possibly from feeder streams, two water courses meeting, weirs or fast-flowing rivers that pass a large bay or obstacle such as a fallen tree. The ensuing effect is that of a whirlpool, the outer edges of which become quite slow or even completely slack. Fish often select these areas to avoid the effort of navigating the main stream and to rest. Food presented to them here, because of the ease with which they can take it, is likely to be of great attraction.

Weir pools, particularly large ones, offer a similar facility. Some of these can provide the equivalent of small, still ponds at the edges of their outflows.

The point at which two rivers converge or a back stream rejoins the main river is known as a confluence. There are areas at the junction of these where you'll find slack water and very probably fish resting or lying in wait for available food. Often just a few yards downstream from the confluence fish activity is also prevalent because of the sudden profusion of foods provided by the waters combining.

This is also true of feeder streams or inflows from drainage ditches etc. Insect life pours into the main flow of the river and fish will gather just a few yards downstream to feed on it.

Bridge walls and other water edge man-made features can be hot spots for fish activity. Algae and weed collect on these and provide attractive feeding opportunities. A float-fished bait drifting downstream as close as possible to the wall can often prove most productive.

Fallen trees or underwater obstacles are also worth investigation. Again they are areas for algae and weed to adhere which in turn provides food for fish.

Man-made canals are usually of a V cut formation. In these it is more likely to find fish feeding on the lower areas of the walls as opposed to the very floor.

Similar to stillwaters, weeds and reeds offer shade and shelter to a variety of species and also provide feeding opportunities. Barbel, for instance, will lie up in such areas and move out to take an attractive passing morsel. A float rig trotted close to, or even through, these beds can often be effective.

Running water venues offer a wonderful variety of angling interest. Even the same river can provide a completely different scene and style of fishing over a relatively short distance with weir and lock pools, shallow runs, deep slow holes, overhanging trees and shrubs and much more. And nobody in the British Isles has to travel far to be in an idyllic and fascinating fishing environment.

CHAPTER 3
FISH

Shown here are the common features that most species of fish share. Not all fish have all of these features and in any case they will vary in size, shape and colour according to the type of fish, but this illustration covers all possibilities with their appropriate names.

Figure 20 **Features of fish**

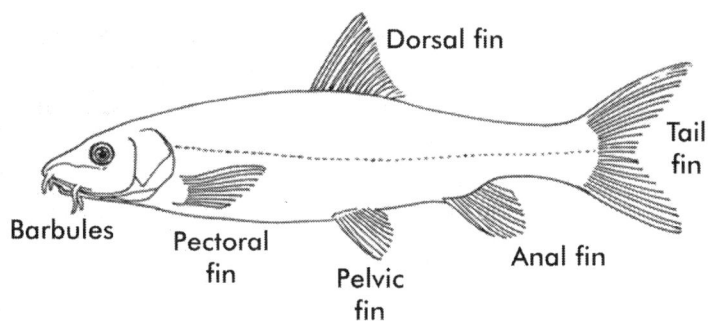

FISH SPECIES
Barbel

A slim, elegant and powerful fish with a greeny brown back and pearl coloured lower half. It is clearly identified by the four barbules – one from each corner of its mouth and two from its snout.

These barbules are designed to feel and smell for food before taking it as the barbel roots about on the river bed. The downward curve of the barbel's mouth is for that purpose. The broad head tapers sharply in a curve to the rounded snout and looking from above the barbel is easy to identify by its wedge shape. When the fish is lying facing into the current in its usual way, the flat underside allows it to lie close to the bottom and the aerodynamic shape of its snout and head pushes the flow of water over it enabling it to retain its position. The dorsal fin is very similar to the upper half of the tail fin and the lower fins are more rounded.

Figure 21 **Barbel**

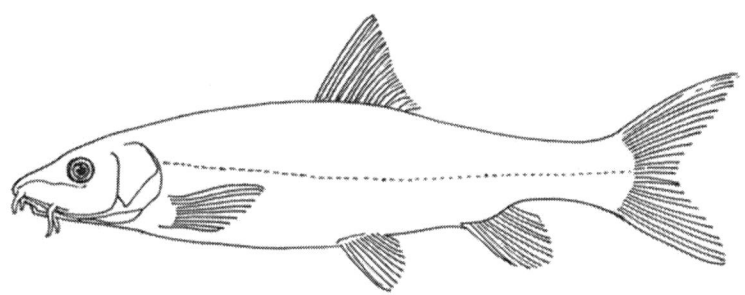

Very young barbel are rarely caught but a year old fish is lightly speckled and resembles its small relation, the gudgeon. An immediately visible difference is the four barbules of the barbel as opposed to the gudgeon's two. By the end of its third year the barbel has grown to around 15" (38cm) and weighs just over 1lb (.45kg). At 7-8 years it will be a powerful 7lbs (3kg) and a superb specimen of 14lbs (6kg) is likely to be 14-15 years old.

Barbel like faster flowing, clean rivers with hard beds. They feed in the layers of silt and mud, weed growth and weed margins. They often live in the thick of the weed feeding on plants and organisms. As they grow they eat minnows, frogs, crayfish, fish fry and snails. Their pharyngeal teeth can deal with crayfish and snails, the shells of which they can eject after extraction of the contents.

Since barbel are bottom feeders ledgering is the answer in deeper waters. Line breaking strain should be at least 6lb (2.7kg) to cope with these powerful fish.

Good general baits include luncheon meat, sausage or maggots. Barbel tend to 'hole up' during the day and fine tackle with small baits are needed if they are to be tempted out. The best times to find feeding barbel are early mornings and the hours either side of dusk. Winter fishing for barbel is the least productive since they prefer the water temperature to be over 7°C.

Bleak

Predominantly found in rivers as opposed to still waters, bleak are slim, silver fish, recognizable by their upturned mouth for surface feeding.

Figure 22 **Bleak**

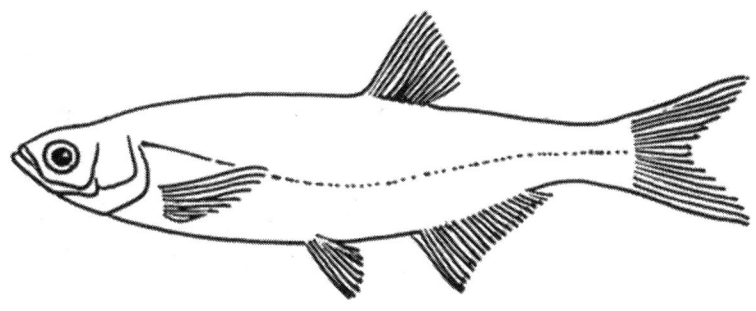

They are normally not much bigger than about 3" (7.5cm) to 4" (10cm) at which size they would weigh around an ounce (28.3g). They can grow to about 8" (20cm) but these are very rare. If you want to fish for them you'll need the lightest and most sensitive float, fine line and tiny hook (18, 20 or 22) baited with a single maggot and fished within a foot or so of the surface.

Bleak are normally considered 'tiddlers' and a nuisance to anglers seeking better quality fish as they can nibble at other float fished baits as they are cast out and begin to sink down through the water. One way to avoid this problem and the ensuing false bites is to weight the line lower down nearer the hook which takes the bait down quicker to the deeper water where the bleak are less likely to follow it.

Bream

There are two varieties of the species – white or silver bream and the common bream.

The **Silver Bream** is much smaller with a maximum size of under 1lb (.45kg). It is bright in colour, very slim and deep in body much like its larger relative the common bream. A distinguishing feature is the scale formation of each side that meet on the underside of the fish in a distinctive V pattern.

These fish are usually found in still water lakes and ponds but occasionally in slow flowing rivers. They tend not to be in large shoals and their feeding habits are not restricted to the bottom. Natural foods include algae, plankton, insect larvae, crustaceans and molluscs. Since they are to be found in still waters and are not necessarily on the bottom,

Figure 23 **Bream**

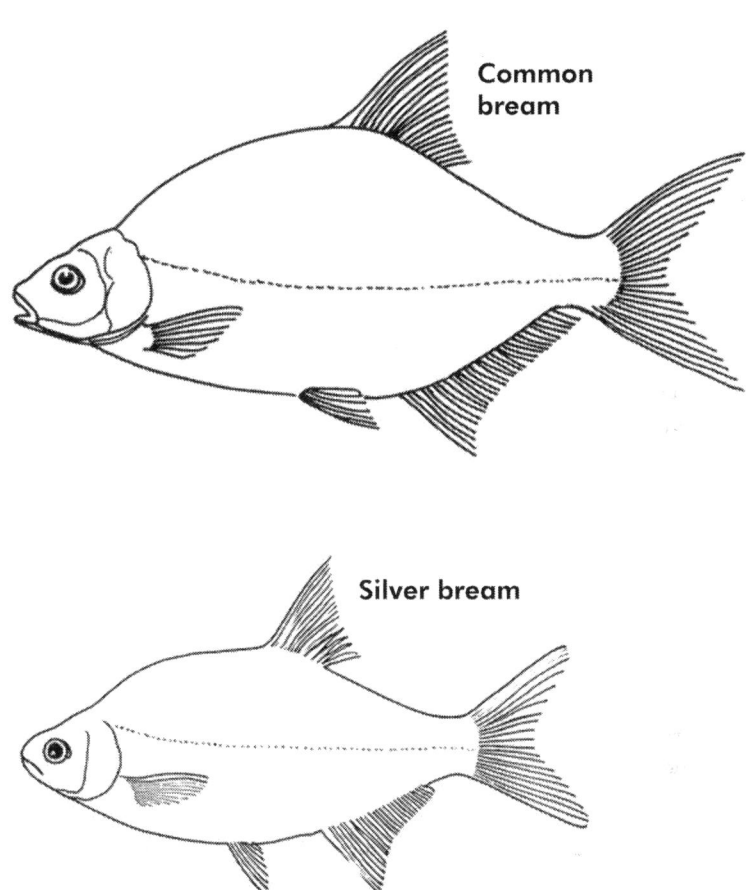

a float fishing rig with light tackle is most probably the best approach.

Maggot, caster or a tiny piece of bread flake are the best baits to employ.

The **Common Bream** is more sought after since it grows to a far more impressive size and is often found in large shoals. Such a shoal, if found to be feeding and fished carefully, will offer a great day's sport. Many experienced anglers who have found such shoals have been known to need two or three keep nets and have weighed in at the end of a session with a total well in excess of 100lbs (45kg).

The common bream has a greeny brown back, golden bronze flanks and a white underside.

They are round backed and deep bodied and weights of around 5lb (2.3kg) are relatively common. Over this and up to 15lb (6.8kg) could be classed as a specimen.

They have small mouths but are at times prolific feeders. They feed on algae, plankton, insect life etc similar to the silver bream. Unlike them, however, the common bream is virtually exclusively a bottom feeder in still waters or sluggish rivers. They tend to be more plentiful in waters in the South of England and are prolific throughout Ireland.

They are often covered in slime and landing and keep nets will need a thorough wash after a successful bream fishing session.

The species tends to lie dormant during winter months and are unlikely to feed unless there is a particularly warm spell of weather. Best times for bream angling are early mornings and dusk during summer months.

When feeding at the bottom a shoal of bream disturb mud, silt and natural gases on the bed of the water. This can cause a visible discolouration of the surface water and also bubbles which could identify a good area to fish. Before feeding, bream will sometimes also roll about on the surface offering a visual indication of the spot to fish.

Ledgering or float fishing can be successfully employed

and the best baits include bread baits, sweetcorn, worms, maggots and casters.

Carp

There are three varieties in the species: Common, Leather and Mirror – which are sufficiently different in appearance to merit individual descriptions.

Common Carp

A fully scaled, deep and full bodied fish with an overall golden colouring. The top of the head and back is a bluish brown, the flanks are golden and the underside is off-white, becoming more yellow towards the rear. The front part of the top fin is tough and almost spiky and care should be taken regarding keep nets since the fish could get hooked into the mesh. Like all varieties of carp it has a very large, rubbery mouth with four barbules – two of them above the upper jaw and one at each corner of the mouth.

Figure 24 **Common carp**

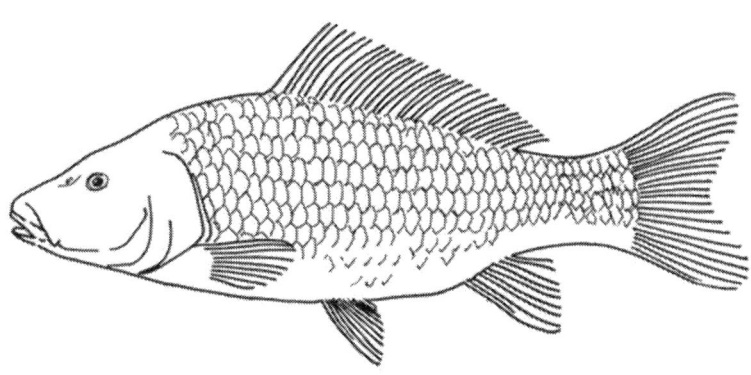

Leather Carp

This variety has no scales at all and thus completely smooth but in virtually every other respect is similar to the Common Carp.

Figure 25 **Leather carp**

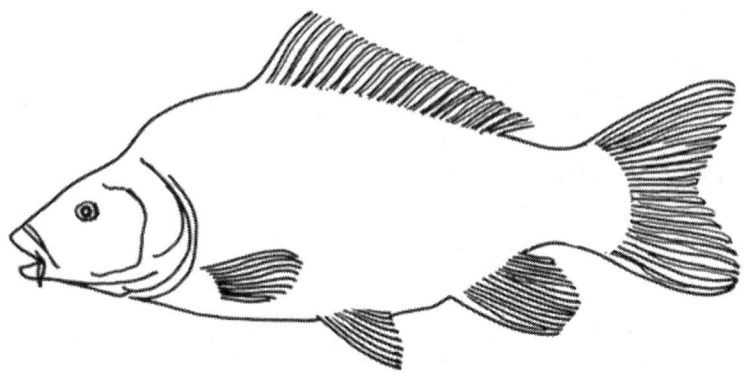

Mirror Carp

Again, similar in most respects to its other two relatives but with the very distinctive feature of the disproportionately large, golden coloured scales generally found along the lateral line as shown in Figure 26.

All of these three species are extremely cunning, hard fighting fish that can grow in the UK to weights in excess of 40lbs (18kg). A fish of 15lbs (6.8kg) or more would generally be classed as a specimen. Normally found in still or sluggish waters they favour more shallow and warmer spots with soft muddy bottoms and a lot of vegetation and aquatic life. Whilst predominantly bottom feeders they will often come to the surface to take a floating morsel.

Figure 26 **Mirror carp**

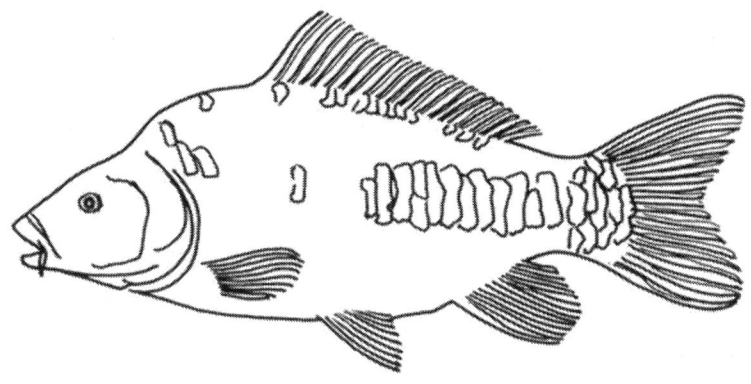

As with bream, bubbles are often tell tale signs as to the position of carp. The fish takes in a mouthful of the mud or silt, extracts what food stuffs it may contain and blows out the rest causing a series of bubbles that rise to the surface.

Carp feed for most of the year but are more voracious during the summer months. They feed throughout the day but the best times to go in search of them are in the early summer mornings, late evening and the first couple of hours of darkness.

Carp accept all manner of baits, some of which to the inexperienced will seem highly unlikely to interest any type of fish. For example, cat and dog foods (plus various mixtures that include them), potatoes, dog biscuits, prawns, cockles, all manner of high protein baits either bought ready made or from recipes you can make yourself, which include strawberry or banana flavours and much more. Carp also take the more traditional baits including maggot, caster, freshwater swan mussels, worms, cheese, sweetcorn, pork luncheon meat and bread baits. These are all usable on ledger or float and a piece of floating crust can be particularly successful when they are surface feeding on a hot summer's day.

Ledger or float can be equally successful but when fishing for big carp it is worth using fairly heavy tackle with breaking strain lines of at least 6lbs (2.7kg) and large hooks. The fish you connect with could well be that sort of weight and they are, in any case, strong fighters. The hook needs to be of optimum sharpness and size is important in view of the carp's big, rubbery mouth from which small hooks will easily come free.

Crucian Carp
These are much less common in England than the other three members of the carp family and are non-existent in Scotland, Ireland and Wales. It is virtually exclusively a stillwater inhabitant and has a preference for heavily overgrown and swampy ponds. It can survive the lower oxygen levels of this type of almost stagnant water better than any other freshwater fish.

It forages in the thick mud and silt feeding off the plant life and will occasionally come to the surface to take water beetles or insect larvae.

When they are surface feeding, freelining techniques including the use of floating crust can be effective. Otherwise a static bait on the bottom using either float or ledger method can do the trick. Bread baits, worms, maggots, luncheon meat, dog or cat foods are recommended baits.

Crucians feed more prolifically in warmer temperatures and fishing the early morning or late evening during the summer months is likely to be the most effective.

Figure 27 **Crucian carp**

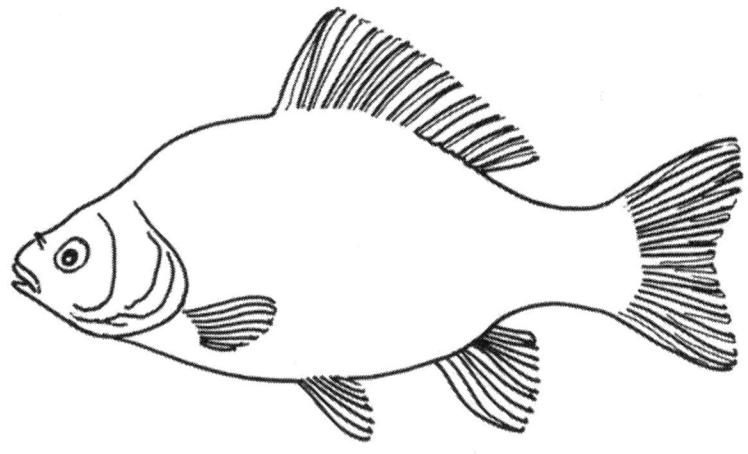

Whilst similar in overall shape and appearance to the other species of carp it doesn't grow as big with a weight of 2lbs (.9kg) being quite a good specimen. A true crucian has no barbules but cross breeding occurs with common, leather and mirror carp which can result in a hybrid crucian with a single barbule on one side of the mouth. Another distinguishing feature is the pronounced dorsal fin of a convex shape.

The crucian is a dark golden brown with a darker back and lighter underside. The dorsal and tail fins are darker and the pectoral, pelvic and anal fins are orangy red.

Catfish

The Wels catfish is not native to Britain and many attempts have been made to increase the numbers of the species here. It is still rare and only likely to be found where it has been introduced to a coarse fishery.

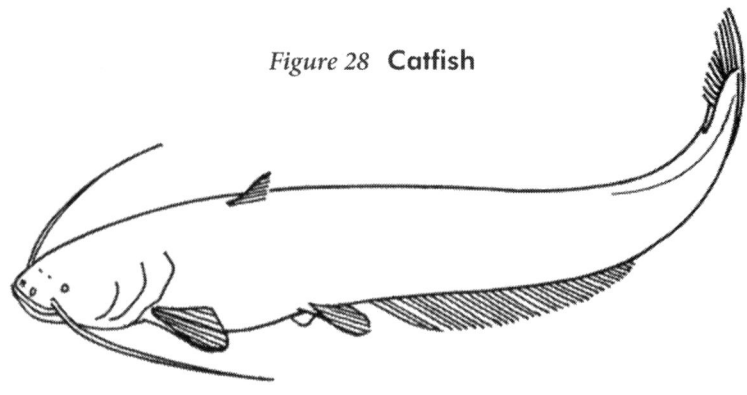

Figure 28 **Catfish**

It has a long sinuous body which is rather flat. The dorsal fin is very small and set well forward. The anal fin is unusually long, as is the tail fin small. The head is short, quite flat and with a hugely wide mouth. The long barbules may well account for it being christened the 'cat' fish since they operate rather like a cat's whiskers in that they feel and avoid obstacles. They are also very sensitive in smelling for food.

Since this species is so unlike any other British coarse fish, should you ever catch one it is unlikely that you wouldn't immediately identify it.

The catfish is a slow and lazy fish and is most likely to feed on deadbaits such as gudgeon or roach or freshwater swan mussels. They are largely summer feeders and will feed at virtually any time of day or night whilst temperatures are reasonably high. If you are planning to fish for them ensure that you are using heavy duty tackle, strong line and large hooks. Wels catfish in England have not reached the massive weights of some of those found in other countries, but one of 40lbs (18kg) plus is not beyond the realms of possibility.

Chub

Chub belongs to the carp family although it looks distinctly different. The adult chub is a very solid, muscular fish. It has a large rounded head with a big tough mouth and thick lips. Its back is a greeny brown, the flanks silvery and the underside a whitish yellow. It has well defined fins which range from colourless to red on more mature fish. Small chub are easily confused with dace but a good method of distinction is by the fins. The chub has large fins with rounded convex rear edges – the dace concave rear edges.

Figure 29 **Chub**

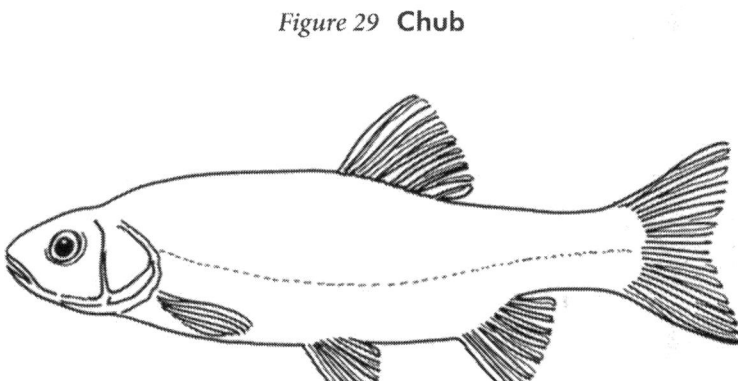

A good sized chub is between 3lb and 5lb (1.4-2.3kg) and will give a tremendous battle. Winter chub are in peak condition for an even better tussle.

Whilst occasionally found to a reasonably good size in still waters the chub is much more predominant in rivers, particularly those of gravel or stony beds with faster flowing and cleaner water. When small they are found in shoals sometimes mixed with roach and rudd but the better specimens tend to be more solitary, often in small groups of three or four with the largest leading the pack.

Chub lie up in deeper holes along river margins and an experienced angler will often be able to identify these.

Small chub feed on insects, fish eggs, molluscs and plant life. With a rise in water temperature they can be seen just beneath the surface, head to the current, studying passing food.

Larger specimens eat small fish, flies and anything edible that lands on the surface. They also eat fruit and berries from overhanging bushes and at the right time of the year, in the right location, an elderberry or blackberry as a hook bait can be very effective.

Crayfish, swan mussels and small frogs are also part of a larger chub's diet.

Many baits will interest chub. Cheese, sweetcorn, brandling, worm, maggot and caster are popular, but fruit, berries, slugs and natural or artificial flies are useful too. Larger specimens will also fall to a spoon or other artificial lure used when spinning.

Chub feed mostly at the bottom except in summer or when the water temperature is high, so you can ledger or float fish according to the conditions.

Dace

Exclusively a river dweller, dace prefer fast moving, well oxygenated waters and are generally found close to the surface. They are essentially shoal fish but the better specimens tend to be found in isolation. They are a small slim species and a fish of 8oz (227g) would be a good specimen catch. They are of an olive colour along the back, the sides are bright silver and the underside is white. Dace can be mistaken for small chub as described in the chub section above but are identifiable by the concave curve in the back edge of the fins as opposed to the convex shape of those of the chub.

Figure 30 **Dace**

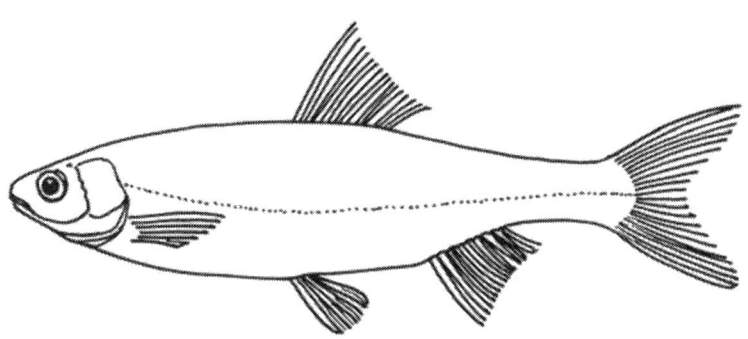

The natural diet is mostly insects and aquatic plant life and they feed at all levels depending on temperature and water conditions.

Dace will take bread baits, hemp, wheat, elderberry, maggot or casters, caddis flies, woodlice, freshwater shrimps or worms.

Ledger or float can be employed and the correct uses of small handfuls of groundbait on a regular basis will help keep the shoal in your vicinity.

Eel

Needs very little description as it is hardly likely to be mistaken for anything else. With the exception of the small pectoral fins at the gills, all the other fins are joined together to form one long fin that runs most of the length along the top and underside. Very young eels, known as elvers, grow into yellow eels which are brownish yellow, darker down the length of the back. A fully mature eel, shortly before it makes the journey back to the Sargasso Sea to spawn from which it never returns, has by then become a silvery colour. The females grow larger than the males and can achieve a length of 4 feet (1.2m) with reported weight of up to 20lbs (9kg).

Figure 31 **Eel**

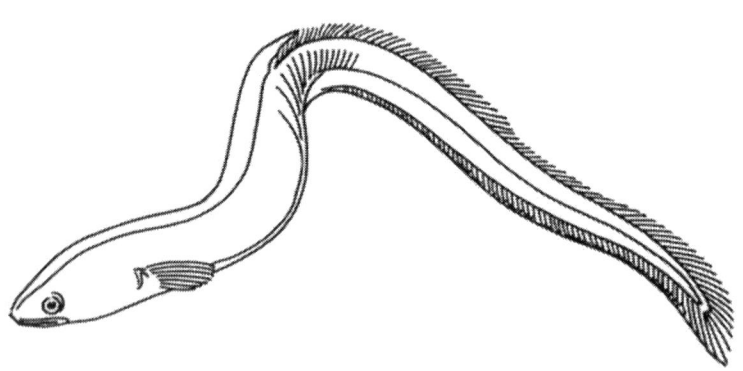

Eels can be found in most still waters and slow flowing rivers. They are exclusively bottom feeders living off almost anything of animal origin, alive or dead. They are largely summer feeders and tend to begin feeding as night falls. Baits such as worm, a cluster of maggots or small dead baits will bring success if eel fishing. The use of strong breaking strain line is important since eels tend to curl up, wrapping themselves round underwater weed or obstacles, and can put up a fight comparable to a fish three times their weight. Because of their tendency to vacuum up the food they take, all too often they will swallow the hook beyond the safe use of a disgorger. When this happens it is recommended to cut the line as close to the mouth as possible and release the fish back to the water where it will hopefully wriggle the hook free.

If you are fishing on the bottom at nightfall for other species and there is a known presence of eels it is advisable to change bait to something less attractive to the eel such as bread and high protein baits, cheese or sweetcorn. There is nothing more frustrating than having to deal with an unwanted eel in failing light and in all probability having to re-tackle afterwards. On a water where there have hitherto been no sign of bream, carp or tench bubbles, a night time run of small bubbles along the surface could well indicate the presence of eels.

Grayling

A long, slim fish, readily identified by its enormous dorsal fin and the unusual feature of a tiny fin on its back known as the adipose, situated close to the tail fin.

Figure 32 **Grayling**

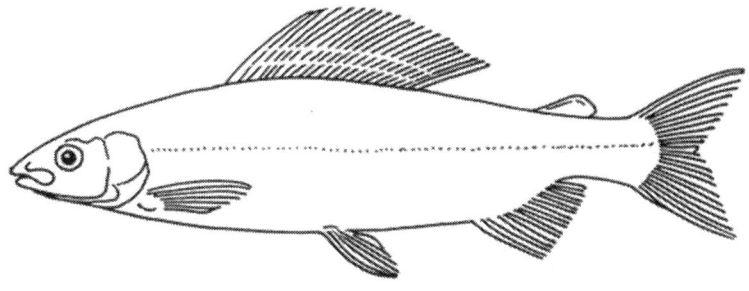

Whilst distributed throughout the British Isles, the grayling only survives in the purest and most oxygenated waters such as fast, gravel bottomed rivers.

Its natural diet includes aquatic insect life, shrimps, snails, fish fry and small fish. Best baits are brandling worms, maggot and wasp grubs.

A good specimen would be around 2lbs (.9kg).

Gudgeon

A tiny relative of the barbel, it is readily distinguishable from other small coarse fish by its mottled greenish yellow speckles along its flanks. It is virtually straight from mouth to tail and it has two barbules – one at each corner of its mouth.

Figure 33 **Gudgeon**

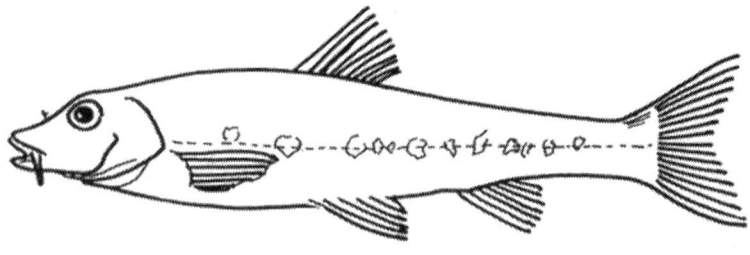

Gudgeon are rarely more than 2 or 3oz (56-85g) and are often a nuisance when fishing for larger, more interesting species. They are exclusively bottom feeders, eating minute organisms. They prefer gravel or sandy bottomed running waters but can withstand high levels of pollution and are found in virtually every waterway, feeding all year round.

Should you choose to fish for gudgeon, baits to use are maggot, caster or brandling using a float or ledger with bait on, or very close to, the bottom.

Perch

Certainly the most colourful and striking freshwater fish. Darkish olive green along its back and off-white on its underside with distinctive vertical, pointed dark stripes along its body. The pelvic, anal and lower part of the tail fin are orangy red – often very bright in colour. The front dorsal fin is a dark olive colour with a tough series of spines and, on a good specimen, an area to be avoided when holding the fish since they are unpleasantly sharp! The scales have tiny spikes on the edges which give the fish an overall rough feel. Perch are bold, fierce and have a voracious appetite often taking baits much too large for their size. Small ones of up to 3" to 4" (7-10cm) feed off crustaceans and a variety of insect life and as they grow so does their appetite for fish fry. Larger specimens will take a variety of small fish including baby perch.

Figure 34 **Perch**

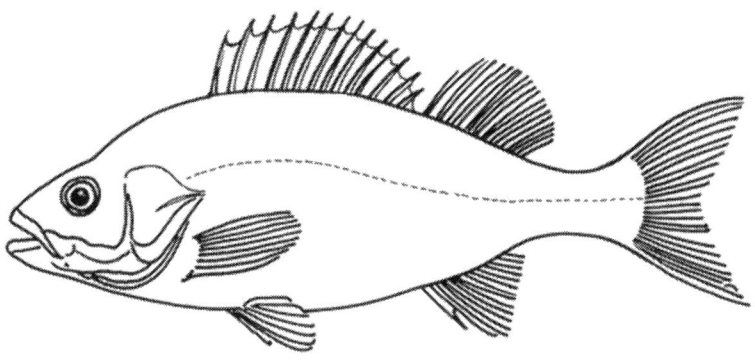

They can be found in most still and moving waters, are often in shoals and feed year long.

The perch is predominantly a bottom feeder and good baits include lob worm, earthworm, maggot and caster. Where fishing for really good specimens of, say, 2lbs to 3lbs (.9-1.4kg), dead baits of small fish such as minnow are effective as is spinning with artificial lures or spoons.

Perch rarely grow to more than around 4lbs (1.8kg) and one of 1lb (.45kg) is a good fish.

Float or ledger tackle can be employed with baits set close to, or on, the bottom.

Pike

Designed by nature for one specific purpose – to be a killer. From a very young age they kill other fish and, indeed, each other. As they grow, so does their voracious appetite. An adult pike will attack another twice its size without regard to the consequences and big pike will hunt water rats, voles, mice, frogs, ducklings and moorhens. It is not uncommon for a large pike to stalk a moorhen with her trailing line of chicks and pick off the last in the line.

Figure 35 **Pike**

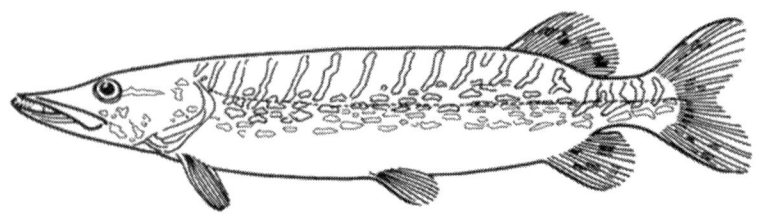

The pike has a huge mouth, formed by crocodile-like jaws. The mouth and jaws are full of razor sharp teeth and even the tongue is armed with them. Once a victim is in the vice like grip of its mouth, there is no escape.

It has a long, torpedo shape with enormous strength and speed over short distances. The power of its tail and tail fin provide lightning acceleration and turning ability. It is an olive bronze along the back with lighter flanks, blotched with cream spots which provide a most effective camouflage while it lies in wait for its prey. Its underside is off-white and virtually flat to allow it to remain flat on the bed of water margins out of sight.

The fins are large in proportion to its shape and are usually orange in colour, with dark markings.

The lifespan of the pike is long and they continue to grow over their many years. Many specimen catches of 40lbs (18kg) plus have been recorded over the years and a good weight and exciting catch for a beginner would be anything over 5lbs (2.3kg).

Pike thrive in all types of water. Ponds, lakes, streams, rivers, gravel pits and reservoirs throughout the British Isles all hold them. Big pike will be found wherever there are good sized shoals of fish for food.

They feed virtually all year round although their food requirements lessen during the really cold weather when their metabolic needs are reduced and they tend to lie more dormant.

Good times for fishing for them are early morning and late evening when they will be in search of food during a period of 1 to 2 hours. Basically the pike is an idle fish that prefers to lie hidden, ready to pounce on a closely passing sick fish that requires little effort to catch, but there are times when it goes into frenzied action attacking shoals.

It can be a nuisance to anglers who have been carefully groundbaiting a swim and have successfully attracted shoals of other feeding coarse fish when a hungry pike roams into the midst of them, scattering them and spoiling the fishing.

Methods of fishing for them include float fishing with a dead coarse fish as bait, presented at virtually any depth. A special large float known as a bung is employed along with heavy breaking strain line. Other dead baits can be mackerel strips, herrings or sprats.

Spinning is effective using artificial lures, spoons and plugs and a particularly lethal lure is one that strongly resembles a sick fish when retrieved through the water with a 'sink and draw' method, discussed in a later section on spinning in Chapter 4.

Whatever method you employ, you should always use a wire trace between the end of the reel line and the bait or lure since the pike's teeth could easily sever nylon, whatever its strength!

One final word of warning. You could find yourself battling with a pike when you are not fishing for them since it is not unknown for one to take a coarse fish in the process of being played or landed. The design of the pike's mouth and array of teeth is such that when locked around its prey it is difficult to be released. There are stories of anglers fishing for small roach who have ended up landing double figure pike as well.

Roach

Often the first species of coarse fish to be caught by the beginner, due to the vast numbers to be found in nearly all still and running waters throughout the British Isles.

Figure 36 **Roach**

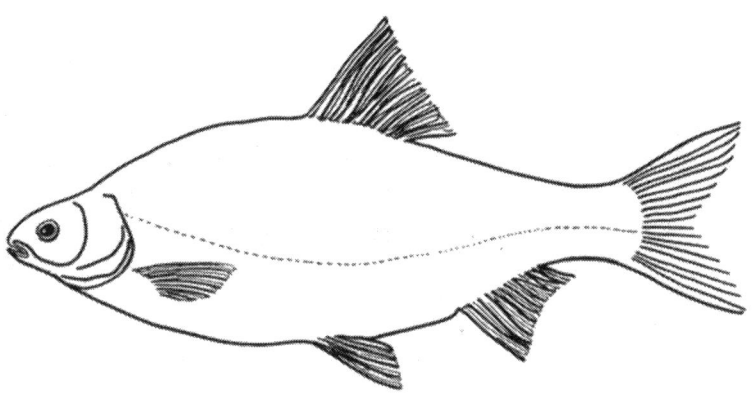

The roach is greyish blue along its back, with flanks of bright silver and an underside of pale cream. The mouth is small and round and its fins are dull red. It is often confused with rudd but distinguishable differences are the more vibrant red of the fins of the rudd, the rudd's protruding lower jaw and its dorsal fin positioned further back than that of the roach.

Roach do not grow large compared to various other species and a fish of 2lbs (.9kg) is an excellent specimen. They swim and feed in large shoals, sometimes as many as several hundred and their natural foods include insect life and aquatic vegetation, small water snails, bloodworms and fish fry.

Roach feed throughout the year and will take maggots, casters, bread baits, hemp, sweetcorn and worms. They are largely bottom feeders but in summer will come to the surface to feed on insects.

Float or ledger can be used but roach are shy feeders, so fine and light tackle should be employed with care to avoid vibrations or splashes.

Rudd

Considered by some to be one of the prettiest shoaling coarse fish. Compared to its body size the head is very small. The fish is slim with an olive coloured back and bright golden flanks that fade to a pale cream underside. The pectoral, dorsal and tail fins are a brownish red and the pelvic and anal fins are usually a brilliant red. The fish has an overall smooth, glossy sheen.

Figure 37 **Rudd**

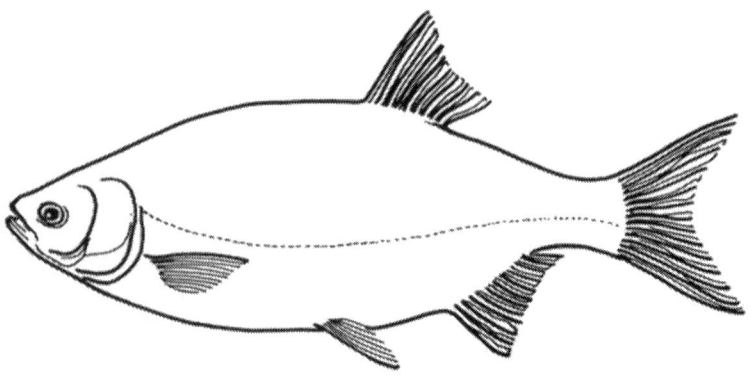

Rudd are easily confused with roach and the clearest means of identification are its brilliant colouring, a bottom jaw set forward as in other upward feeding fish such as the bleak and the position of its dorsal fin which is set further back than that of the roach.

Rudd are normally inhabitants of stillwater ponds and lakes but can occasionally be found in sluggish rivers. They feed largely on insect life at the surface but should this become insufficient during the winter months they will sometimes turn their attention to the bottom where they will forage in silt and vegetation.

The method of fishing for them is almost certainly with a float, probably fished shallow with very fine light tackle, small hook and small baits such as a single maggot, caster or a tiny piece of bread flake.

Ruffe

The ruffe is a small relation of the perch and shares its

Figure 38 **Ruffe**

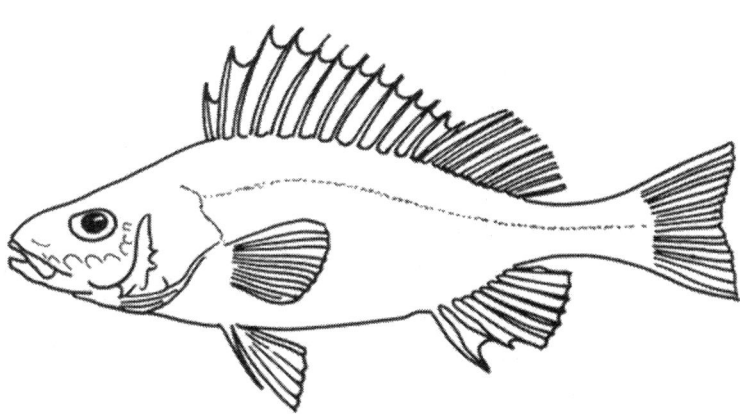

voracious appetite, albeit on a much smaller scale. It has a similar shape to the perch including the spiky dorsal fin and a large mouth in relation to its body size. It has a greenish grey colouring with dark blotches along its flanks. It seems to have an overall slightly transparent look and rarely grows to more than 3" to 4" (7-10cm) in length.

The ruffe, or pope as it is otherwise known, has a habit of lunging hungrily at a bait and if you are not fast to strike, it will often have swallowed the bait and will need the use of a disgorger.

Since it is unlikely that you will want to fish specifically for this species we have confined this section to its identification only.

Tench

Tench are a thick set species with a humped back that slopes up from the rounded head. It has tiny eyes and thick rubbery lips with a small barbule either side. It has an olive coloured back and greenish golden flanks. All of its fins have rounded edges and the whole fish is covered in a thick slime that obscures its covering of tiny scales. The underside is a cream colour and is virtually flat as in the nature of so many bottom feeders.

Tench grow to in excess of 12lbs (5kg) but a fish of 3lbs (1.4kg) or more is a good specimen. Related to the carp family they are hard fighting fish that give anglers excellent sport in playing and landing.

Predominantly found in stillwaters and slow flowing canals and rivers, they remain in large shoals whilst small, gradually reducing in shoal size as they increase in size and weight. When they attain weights in excess of around

Figure 39 **Tench**

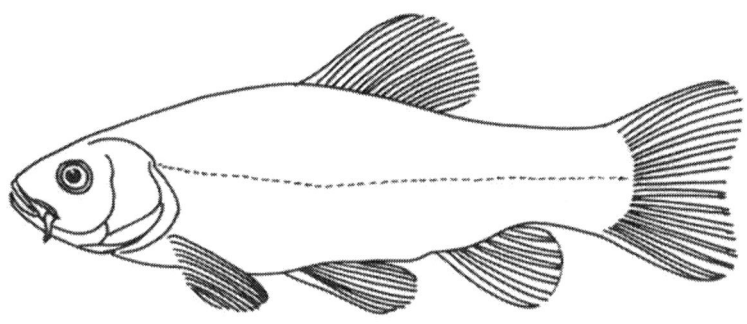

7lbs (3kg), they are to be found in small groups, sometimes even just cruising in pairs. As a preferred habitat the thicker the mud, silt and vegetation the better. Adult tench feed on crustaceans, molluscs, water snails and insect life on the bed of the water. Like the carp their activities in foraging in the mud give tell-tale patterns of bubbles on the surface to identify where they are feeding.

The tench is basically a summer feeder and the most successful times to fish for them are early mornings or late evenings through the summer to mid autumn. Winter tench are usually few and far between particularly after the beginning of frosts when they will remain dormant until the spring.

Whilst they will occasionally come to the surface for insect activity or feed mid-water, the bottom is the place to fish for them. Ledgered or float fished baits such as bread, sweetcorn, worms, black slugs, snails, maggots and casters are favourite and, by whatever method, the tench bite is usually firm and positive.

Tench will leave considerable slime on landing and keep

nets which will need a thorough clean after a session to avoid stiff, dry and encrusted mesh that will also smell quite unpleasant unless you are using the rubber mesh types mentioned earlier on.

Zander

The largest and most spectacular of the perch family, it is clearly recognisable as a relation because of its dorsal fins. The front is spiky with 14 sharp, tough rays and the rear dorsal is long and soft and of a convex shape. The body of the fish is long and muscular and resembles that of the pike although the jaws are somewhat smaller. However, what they lack in size is more than compensated by their power and the size of the long sharp teeth they contain.

Figure 40 **Zander**

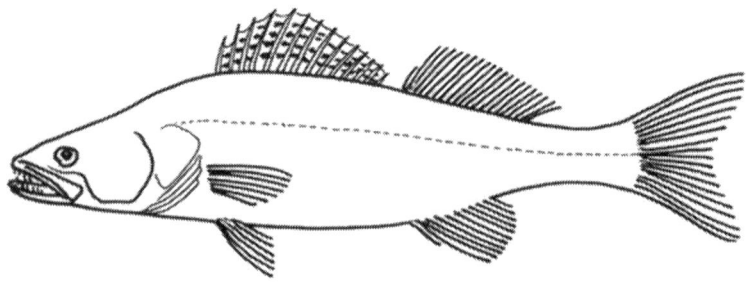

The zander is of a silvery appearance when young, particularly along its flanks which turn to a greenish gold with maturity. The back of an adult fish is a dark olive and the underside almost white. The tail fin is dark while the pectoral, pelvic and anal fins are off-white.

Zander thrive in large, well oxygenated waters such as reservoirs, gravel pits and bigger rivers. They are largely to be found in East Anglia although over recent years have been introduced to other waters in different counties.

The young zander can be found in large shoals which reduce in size as the fish increase in weight until eventually very large, old zander are found in isolation.

Natural foods for them are from shrimps and mussels, to any coarse fish – and, of course, each other!

Unlike pike they tend to stick to more manageable sized meals and take fish either by the head or tail and do not turn them to be able to swallow, as do pike.

Zander see better in the twilight hours and therefore tend to feed at these times, so dawn and dusk fishing is ideal throughout most of the year with the exception of particularly cold snaps.

Like pike they can be float fished with deadbaits but zander as a rule do not take anything other than coarse fish so eliminate mackerel strip, herring, sprat and the like.

If spinning for them bear in mind the smaller mouth and eating habits and stick to smaller lures, spoons and plugs.

A zander of over 10lbs (4.5kg) is an excellent specimen but pound for pound against other species of coarse fish they do not put up much of a fight once hooked.

Very small species

There are a few other species that haven't been described here since they are tiny and you are more likely to catch them when 'dipping' with a shrimping net than with a rod and line.

These are the bullhead, spined/stone loach, minnow and stickleback.

CHAPTER 4
METHOD

CASTING

It is more than likely that once you have tackled up and are poised to make your first cast it will be apparent what you need to do to send your float and bait out onto the water but the basic principles are as follows.

Holding the rod by the upper section of the butt with the foot of the reel between your fingers, release the bail arm, hooking the line over the index finger of the hand holding the reel.

Lift the rod up and out behind you to an angle of some 30 degrees from vertical. The float should be hanging about one foot below the top ring of the rod. Ensure that the line will be sufficiently well away from potential hazards such as branches above you or bushes behind, when you cast.

Then swing the rod over in an arc towards the water. When some 45 degrees from the vertical towards the water release the line hooked over your finger. At this point you will have achieved optimum momentum to project the float tackle out onto the water. With practice you'll soon learn the amount of effort required to achieve long or short distance castings to place the float in your chosen swim.

Underarm casting for short distances is achieved by lifting the rod and swinging the line from in front of you creating a pendulum motion. Using the same technique as mentioned above release the line when you feel the greatest momentum of the tackle has been achieved. Either of these methods are also used when ledgering.

FLOATS AND SHOTTING

The first basic principle is to weight any type of float so that as little as possible is above the water level but not so little that you cannot easily see it or detect any movement of it. The less of it there is above the water, the less resistance the fish will feel when it takes the bait.

On arrival at a water that is new to you, assess the conditions prevailing and select the appropriate float as outlined here.

Stick Float

This is fixed to the line at top and bottom of the float and is useful on a flowing river as it has the effect of causing the bait to drift at the speed of the water flow and not the surface wind. Shot should not be placed close to the float as this can cause the hook length of line below it to get caught around the float when casting so that it cannot cock. On slow flowing waters shot can be spaced down the hook length with the weight of shot decreasing down the line. The smallest shot should be no closer than 4" to 6" (10-15cm) from the hook.

To get a bait down to the bottom quickly in faster water the bulk of the weight of shot should be placed lower down the line.

Where there is a reasonable flow the line will obviously never hang directly vertically under the float. Thus to keep a bait on the bottom the float should be positioned sufficiently overdepth to compensate for the angle at which the hook length is being carried.

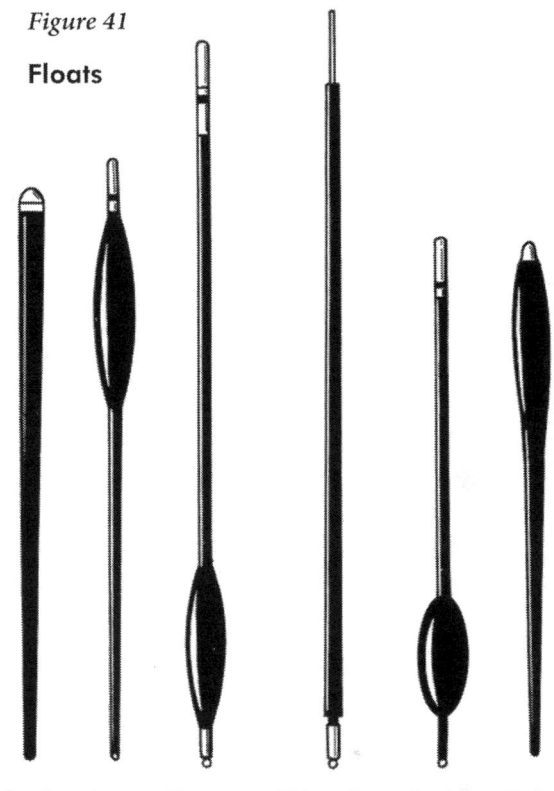

Figure 41

Floats

Stick Avon Zoomer Waggler Onion Balsa

Avon

The avon is attached to the line at both ends of the float. It has a bulbous section towards the top made from balsa wood, giving it greater buoyancy. It is because of this buoyancy that the avon is ideally suited for fishing fast or turbulent water such as a weir pool.

Zoomer

The principle and technique of this is virtually identical to the waggler, the difference being that it is usually larger and weighted at the base to enable greater distance casting for lake or gravel pit fishing.

Waggler

This has a ring at the bottom end through which the line is passed and a shot fixed either side leaving an inch or so between them. The bottom one stops the float sliding down to lower weights or the hook when casting, the upper one is pulled down against the float ring when a fish takes the bait thus pulling the float down and registering the bite.

The waggler is mainly used for stillwaters or very slow flowing rivers.

On a windy day when line between rod tip and float can be blown sufficiently to pull the float out of position, the waggler is useful since it is possible to sink the line. This is achieved by casting further than you need, submerging the rod tip in the water and then retrieving the line to bring the float back to the required position.

Lift the rod tip up to an inch or so above the surface. The line, since only fixed at the bottom of the float, will remain submerged and unaffected by wind.

This type of float offers excellent versatility. Fishing 'on the drop' is a method to send the bait very slowly and naturally down through the water, attracting fish virtually from the surface or those feeding at various depths, down to the bottom feeders. If, using the waggler, the majority of the shotting is placed immediately under the float it will cock immediately leaving the bait with only a dust shot a few inches from the hook to drift down slowly. Thus positioned, bite detection is possible at any level as the bait sinks.

To take the bait down quickly, place the majority of the shot a good way down the hook length well away from the two shot securing the float but still several inches from the hook.

If waggler fishing for species such as bream, carp or tench that feed nose down on the bottom, the 'lift' method can be useful. The tackle is set so that the lowest weight actually rests on the bottom and big baits such as breadflake or paste, sweetcorn etc lie out horizontally on the final hook length. As the fish sucks the bait upwards the bottom weight is lifted from the bed causing the float to ride up on the water or fall over onto its side.

Onion

Very similar in appearance to the zoomer although the bulbous body at the base is unweighted. Its use is also very similar to the waggler and it is merely a question of the user's preference regarding the balance.

The bulbous body gives the float more stability when fishing in windy conditions.

Balsa

Very similar to the stick float being fixed at both ends but with a slight shoulder and slightly bulkier shape which enables it to ride the current of a medium to fast flowing river without being forced in towards the bank. When shotting a balsa it is worth securing a small split shot directly beneath the float to hold it in position as it can slide down the line when either being cast or when striking a bite.

How the float will react to a bite

This is a very inexact science and we can only outline some of the possibilities.

- The most obvious, the float will suddenly vanish beneath the surface. Often taking you by complete surprise! So never take your eye off the float and always have a hand close to, if not holding, the rod butt ready to strike!
- The float will suddenly lie up flat on the surface which indicates that a fish has lifted the bait upwards.
- It will angle slightly and move away gently, sometimes not going under the surface at all. On still or slow moving water it will be obvious whether this is fish interest.
- On occasions, where the float is running at an angle because of water flow, the angle may suddenly change.
- Any of these movements may well be preambled by tiny twitches of the float, known as 'knocks', when a fish is sampling the bait before taking it.

LEDGER

All of the general equipment used for bite detection when ledgering is covered in Chapter 1. Here we will discuss the methods of tackling up the 'business' end and how the whole rig will operate for you.

The whole purpose of ledgering is to retain a bait firmly on the bottom, as much as possible, depending on the strength of the flow, in the same position. This is obviously achieved by the use of weight. Figure 42 is self explanatory in how to set up terminal tackle.

The reaction of a quiver tip to a bite can be one of several.

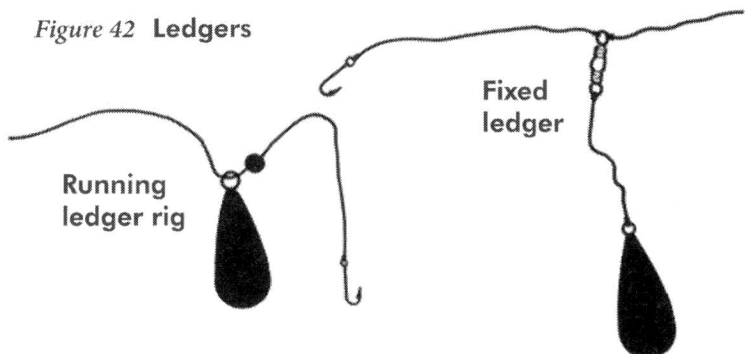

Figure 42 **Ledgers**

It could suddenly slacken if the fish has taken the bait and is swimming toward you. It could jerk violently, swinging the whole rod tip round if it is a solid bite from a powerful fish. Or if it is a cautious fish such as a roach it might, as the name suggests, simply quiver.

Depending on wind, water flow, species of fish and their feeding habits at the venue, when to strike can only be learned with practice. As a rule of thumb for a beginner, strike whenever there is a positive movement that is clearly not caused by extraneous circumstances such as wind that may move the rod tip, passing leaves on the water that have knocked against the line, the movement of the ledger weight rolling along the bottom in a strong flow, or even a passing fish that may brush against the sub surface line.

When ledgering in stillwater, after casting, the rod should be placed at 90 degrees to where you have cast your bait and the quiver tip should be close to the water to reduce any movement of it caused by wind. On moving water such as rivers, the quiver tip should be pointing in the direction of your cast but lifted and creating tension between the tip and your weight and bait which will reduce the effect on the line from any current.

Bobbins, monkey climbers and electronic bite detectors are all versions of bite detection methods in ledgering and are described in Chapter 1.

THE DISGORGER

A most crucial part of your tackle! This is a small slender rod of moulded plastic or pressed aluminium about the size of a slim pencil. An advantage of the plastic variety is that should you drop it into the water it will float so that you can retrieve it. At its head, as shown below, is a slot into which the hook line is inserted before sliding the disgorger into the fish's mouth. Keeping the line reasonably taut the disgorger is slid down the line until it comes into contact with the top end of the hook. Then, once the hook shank is secure in the head of the disgorger, simply push and twist and the hook should come free. The

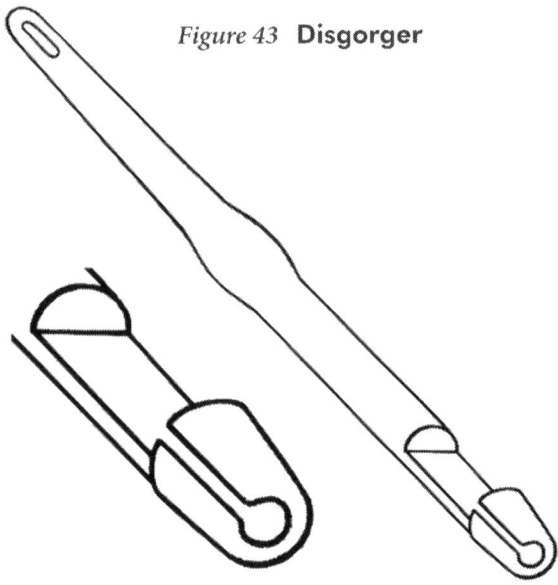

Figure 43 **Disgorger**

technique may take a little getting used to but the secret is not to panic, be gentle and careful and you will very quickly see what an efficient tool this is for removing deeply bedded hooks without damaging the fish. For maximum speed and ease of use, do ensure that you keep two or three disgorgers (they cost very little) in different sizes according to the hook size you may be using.

PLUMMETING

This is important when float fishing an unfamiliar water. Tackle up completely, including the hook. Pass the hook through the ring at the top of the plummet and embed it

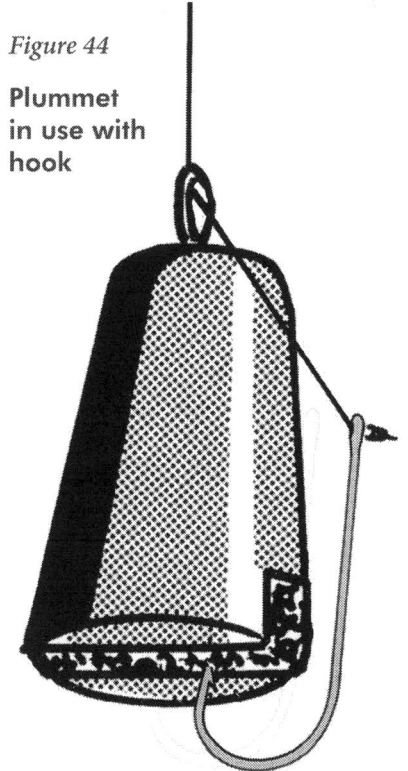

Figure 44

Plummet in use with hook

into the cork at the base of the plummet. Very gently, in order not to frighten fish that may already be feeding your chosen swim, swing the plummet out to where you plan to fish. Should the float disappear beneath the surface, retrieve and slide it further up the line. Conversely, should it lie flat you have set it too deep, so slide it down. You will probably need a few experiments but what you are aiming to achieve is a situation where the float is sitting upright, thus giving you a pretty accurate indication of the depth of water. It is often worth doing this at varying points around your chosen swim as it may show you that there are ledges or deep holes very close to it that otherwise you would not discover.

It is worth a few minutes of plummeting at the outset as this method of 'reading the water' may dramatically improve your day's sport.

DEADBAITING

Used for the four predatory fish species – eel, perch, pike and zander. The types of deadbait are detailed under each in

Figure 45 **Hooking of deadbait**

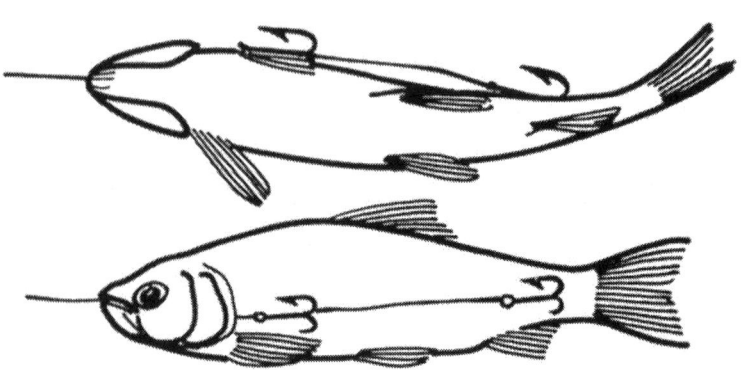

Chapter 3 on types of fish. Figure 45 shows a method of applying the deadbait to the treble hooks.

SPINNING

The principle is to cast out an artificial lure which, when retrieved, will fool a fish into believing it is a ready meal. There are three main types of lures – the spinner, the spoon and the plug.

The Spinner – is a metal blade which, when retrieved through the water, spins rapidly around a metal or wire bar. This bar, to which the treble hook is attached, is adorned in a variety of colours and styles as is the blade so that the visual effect is a small glittering shape moving through the water.

There are various methods of retrieval but it is fun to experiment yourself as you imagine the course of this 'toy' fish you are controlling.

Figure 46 **Spinner**

The 'sink and draw' method is to retrieve quite quickly for several feet and then to give the lure a sharp little tug so that it twitches. After which stop reeling in for a second or two, thus allowing the lure to flutter down deeper through the water. If a fish has been following, it may take the bait at this point. If not, continue the retrieval, bringing the lure glittering up through the water toward you – again for a few feet. Continue this start/stop process to the water's edge.

The Spoon – made of metal, very often in a fish shape, is available on average in sizes from 2" to 6" (5-15cm). It is of flat metal, curved rather like a conventional household spoon. During retrieval it oscillates or wriggles through the water, causing its highly shiny and brightly coloured surfaces to glitter. It has two useful advantages. Firstly that by experimenting at the water's edge you can establish what speed it sinks through the water. Then, having cast out, wait before beginning retrieval and count the seconds. Thus you will know at what depth you are starting your retrieve and will be able to experiment at various depths. Secondly, spoons are considerably heavier than other types of lure and this gives the best distance casting for large lakes and gravel pits plus the ability to cast directly into a strong wind.

Figure 47 **Spoon**

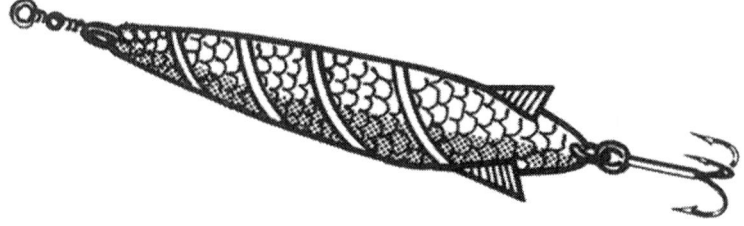

The Plug – This is the favourite lure of the authors because of their successes with it over the years. Plugs are most commonly made from tough plastic or wood. They are designed to resemble and imitate fish. Of the many sizes and patterns available, few accurately resemble any coarse fish but clearly all do the job in fooling the predators. They come in four basic types designed for fishing at various depths in the water.

Figure 48 **Plug**

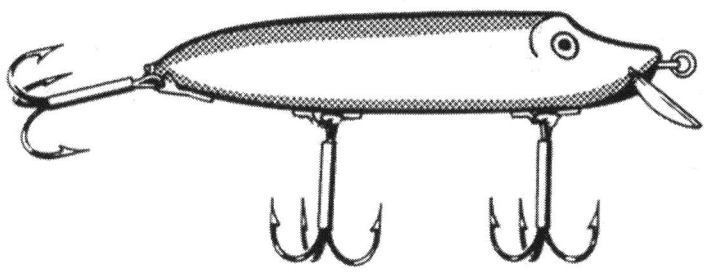

Surface Plugs – wriggle and splash along the surface during retrieval. It is even possible to buy a Mouse or Frog lure of this type which you may wish to experiment with later on.

Floating and Diving Plugs – These are designed with a flat, curved or V shaped piece of plastic inserted into the head of the lure, protruding at an angle, rather like a spade. It is this that causes the diving action. On casting, the plug will float on the water and as you retrieve will plough through it at a gentle angle. The longer and faster you retrieve, the deeper the plug will go until a situation is reached when the angle of your line and the plug's proximity to you dictates it must start to come up towards you. Throughout retrieval the lure wriggles – very like a sick fish – and in some types there is a tiny steel ball within it that rattles, causing vibration that gains the attention of the fish.

With these lures you can employ the 'sink and draw' techniques already described, although in this instance when you stop the retrieve the plug will weave and roll up through the water strongly resembling a dying fish. When you begin to retrieve again it ploughs down as if it has just regained a little strength.

Sinking Plugs – Used for fishing large lakes or gravel pits where distance is required and where there is very deep water and the lure needs to sink a good distance before you can begin your retrieve. These types are larger and heavier and are also often fitted with a steel ball inside to create a vibration.

Deep Diving Plugs – Similar to the floating and diving plugs, these will float when cast but are fitted with an extra large vane or 'spade' at the head that effects a very steep angle of dive. These also allow you to employ the 'sink and draw' method in greater depths of water.

With both this and the floating and diving plugs you also have useful manoeuvrability with underwater obstacles such as shelves, weed beds, sunken trees, roots etc. If you can assess when the lure is approaching them, simply cease the retrieve so that it floats upwards away from such obstacles and can be slowly and safely retrieved over them.

BAITS

What to use for all species has been discussed in Chapter 3. Most of them are either bought, dug up or collected at the waterside, but breadflake – made from stale, unappetising bread – is effectively free and something you can make in cash saving quantities. Remove the crusts and soak the remainder in cold water until it is moist but still intact. Then squeeze it in a cloth until all water is removed. Next knead it into a firm paste. At this point, should you wish to experiment, you may add a flavouring – i.e. almond, aniseed, banana, custard, sugar etc. The mix can then be stored – preferably not longer than overnight – in an airtight container and will remain fresh and pliable for use.

Crust for floating should come from a fresh loaf, dried crust will be difficult to apply to and keep on the hook.

Dog biscuits, either square or circular, which are also a good cereal bait are pre-prepared at home by drilling a tiny hole through the middle. At the water side, the final section of the hook length is passed through this before the hook is tied on. The biscuit then sits on the hook shank and the outside surface area swells. Over a short distance there is sufficient weight to be able to cast these out as a floating bait.

Another popular cereal bait is the 'boilie' which is available in a whole variety of flavours. These are made in balls through which a hook can be pushed with ease. They are, however, expensive for small quantities.

Figure 49 overleaf shows some common baits and the best methods of attaching them to hooks.

Groundbaits – are used to attract fish to the swim you are

Figure 49 **Hooking of baits**

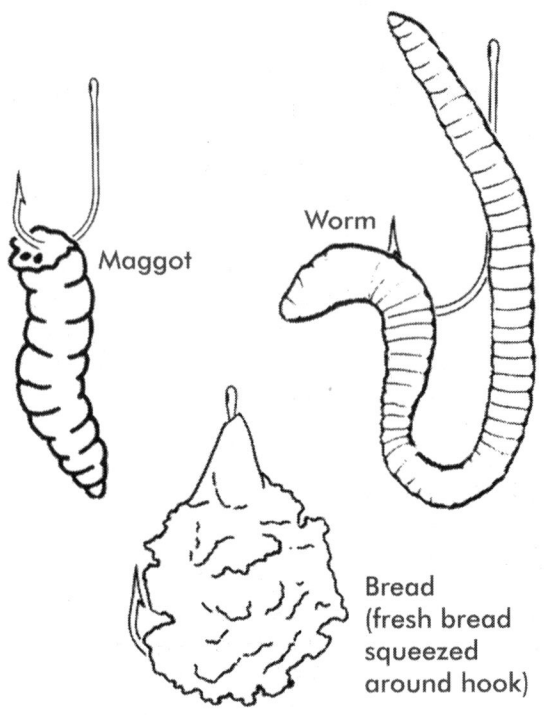

fishing. They can be bought in bags of finely ground grain often with flavourings. These, when mixed with water at the waterside, turn into a paste which is thrown into the swim in balls of 1" to 2" (2.5-5cm) diameter. Some preparations disintegrate on hitting the water to form cloudbait that very slowly drifts down to attract fish at all depths. This is good for stillwaters but in flowing waters a groundbait mix solid enough to sink straight to the bottom before it begins to disperse is better suited. A surface dispersing groundbait would be swept away and, even if you could calculate how far upstream it should be deposited, it would be too widely spread by the time it reached your swim. Groundbait is manufactured for the various types of conditions and species of fish which are featured on the labels of proprietary brands.

Loose baits – i.e. samples of the hook bait being used can also be loose fed into the swim or mixed with the groundbaits mentioned above.

Whatever you are using for groundbait, little and often is the generally accepted rule. Too much and the fish could become too well fed and uninterested in the hook bait. Too little, possibly not applied frequently enough, and fish may swim away to better food sources. This is obviously entirely dependent on the quantity of fish feeding and can only be a matter of trial and error.

'PLAYING' AND LANDING A FISH

Having successfully struck into the fish it will obviously immediately do its best to escape. You must control its first runs by keeping pressure on the line and if necessary allowing it line by using the clutch (as described under Fixed Spool Reels in Chapter 1). Each time the fish slows or pauses to regain energy, reel in line to bring it closer. Should it run towards your bank reel in as fast as possible, if necessary lifting the rod tip high to accommodate slack line that you cannot reel in fast enough.

If it is a good fish that has dived very deep and is beginning to show first signs of tiring it may be 'pumped' back up through the water toward you. Whilst preventing line spooling off, lift the rod high and swiftly reel in the slack line as you do so. Wait to gauge the reaction of the fish and if it makes no powerful attempt to run or dive repeat the action until you have surfaced it. Make no attempt to land it until either its head is clear of the water or it is beginning to roll on its side, tired enough not to protest strongly at the feel or sight of the landing net.

During the 'pumping' process, should it make another aggressive run, allow it controlled line again using the clutch on the reel until you can stop its progress, turn it back to face you and restart the 'pumping'.

When the fish is ready to be landed and whilst several feet away from the bank, slip the landing net quietly and gently into the water as far out as you can comfortably manage. Ensure the entire net and its edge are completely submerged just below the surface. If conditions allow, let go of the landing net handle to be able to reel the fish very close to, if not completely over, the landing net. Then, holding the rod tip high to keep the fish still, regain the landing net handle and lift under the fish. If it is a sizeable fish do not try and lift it using the landing net pole. It will bend unmanageably or, if glass fibre, possibly even snap. Using one hand to keep the rod and tackle away from potential tangle, use the other to bring in the pole bit by bit until you can grab the net rim. At all times be sure not to allow the fish to brush or bump against any obstacles that could damage it.

Lift the fish in the net clear of the water to a place where it can be unhooked comfortably, inspected, weighed, photographed or generally admired. Minimise its time out of the water and gently return it to the water or into a keep net. When returning a fish to the water hold it gently under its belly and lower it down until it is immersed, allowing it to swim quietly away.

CHAPTER 5
HINTS AND TIPS

We have now covered all aspects of tackle, waters, fish, methods and baits to give a good all round basic knowledge for the beginner. The following are a series of notes on other aspects which had no place elsewhere in the book but are nevertheless important.

Carbon Rods/Poles and Lightning

Carbon is an excellent conductor of electricity and at the onset, or even the likelihood, of an electric storm, immediately cease fishing with any carbon material and replace it in the rod bag as soon as possible.

Power Lines

Always take extreme care when using carbon anywhere near them and ensure that there is no way you could cast, miscast or strike up into them.

Sunglasses

Not an imperative item but on glaring, sunny days most comfortable and if float fishing, highly recommended. Polarised glasses are ideal and can even help visibility into the water.

Noise

Excessive noise can disturb other anglers and spoil what should be an idyllically peaceful recreation. It is not noise but vibration on the bankside by footfall or excessive movement on a boat that is quickly transmitted to fish and which will cause them to leave the vicinity.

Shadows/Reflections

If you turn up at a water and suddenly present a huge shadow of yourself or wave an arm across the water you can kiss goodbye to any fish that may have been feeding or cruising near the surface. So stealth is basically the answer and totally crucial. Approach the waterside as quietly and gently as you can. Tackle up away from the water so as not to create bankside vibrations or shadows. Try not to create shadows over the water. Cast out beyond the area you have chosen to fish so as not to disturb fish feeding in your chosen swim and gently bring your bait back to that area.

Licence

Virtually everywhere you can legally fish in England and Wales you will need a rod and line licence if you are aged 12 or older. These can be bought at any main Post Office counter, online at www.environment-agency.gov.uk or by telephone on 0844 800 5386. Spot checks are made frequently by Environment Agency officials and it is always most important that you carry your licence with you when fishing.

Coarse Fishing Season

This runs from 16th June to 15th March inclusive on inland waterways. Fishing on some ponds, lakes and reservoirs is allowed during the close season.

Rubbish

It is imperative to the conservation of countryside, the safety of wildlife and indeed, the continuing angling access to waters, that no line or discarded tackle is ever left at the bankside. Crisp packets, cans, bait wrappers, paper bags etc will all go back into the tackle box with no problem and leave the swim pleasantly ready for other anglers – or even you!

Permissions

It is often necessary to buy a day ticket to fish a water. In many places it can be bought at the bankside when the relevant club's bailiff arrives but it may be necessary to apply for, and receive, your permit before you set out.

If it is not apparent from signage at the waters or from discussion with other anglers, the local tackle shop can normally advise.

Always check the club, society, or management rules on the water you are planning to fish with regard to restrictions on the use of groundbaits, baits, barbed hooks, keep nets and acceptable techniques in general.

And above all keep to the Country Code.

AND FINALLY ...

Coarse angling is a wonderful sport. There are few people who, having taken it up with any degree of sincerity, ever give it up. No matter how long you have been fishing there will always be new things to learn. We hope this little book has set you on that path for a lifetime's fun and fascination.

Printed in Great Britain
by Amazon